King Here

King Here

Never Too **OLD**, Too **RICH** or Too **ANYTHING** to Meet Jesus

Trish Porter Topmiller

NASHVILLE

NEW YORK • LONDON • MELBOURNE • VANCOUVER

King Here

Never Too Old, Too Rich or Too Anything to Meet Jesus

Published in New York, New York, by Morgan James Publishing. Morgan James is a trademark of Morgan James, LLC. www.MorganJamesPublishing.com

The Morgan James Speakers Group can bring authors to your live event. For more information or to book an event visit The Morgan James Speakers Group at www.TheMorganJamesSpeakersGroup.com.

ISBN 9781642791198 paperback
ISBN 9781642791204 eBook
Library of Congress Control Number: 2018947239

Cover and Interior Design by:
Chris Treccani
www.3dogcreative.net

In an effort to support local communities, raise awareness and funds, Morgan James Publishing donates a percentage of all book sales for the life of each book to Habitat for Humanity Peninsula and Greater Williamsburg.

Get involved today! Visit
www.MorganJamesBuilds.com

My gift to my kids and my grandchildren: honesty,
wisdom, and love.
Chuckism

To all those who knew Chuck King—the dad, grandfather, entrepreneur, workaholic, giver, adventurer, adrenal junkie, and opioid statistic. This is for those who didn't know the final story of how he met an "angel," changed, and finished his life worshipping the Lord Jesus Christ.

To all those who think it's not possible for someone to come to know the Lord because they're either too old, too rich, or too . . . anything. Whatever it is.

To all those whose lives aren't done yet (that's you if you're reading this), know that your life is like a puzzle and each piece fits together. In the end it forms an amazing picture. Often, it doesn't look how we thought it would. Please know that you are loved, valuable, and important!

"Look at the nations and watch—
and be utterly amazed. For I am
going to do something in your
days that you would not believe."

(Hab. 1:5)

Thank You

It's the little things in life that count.
Chuckism

This story is made up of people, and there are many to thank.

Charlie, Mike, Leslie, and Annalisa, who spent countless hours responding to so many of Dad and Debe's needs over the years and dealt with them on a regular basis. I am so proud and grateful to have you as my brothers and sisters-in-law. Thank you for your feedback, photos, and help with Dad's story.

Dad's close friends, Tom Sorenson, Dan Newby, and James Dalton, who filled in a few blanks and added life to several of Dad's adventures. It was fun growing up with you. You are so special to me and my dad. Thank you.

Beth Ann, who was a shining light in Dad's and all our lives. You were a godsend!

Angela, I appreciate all you do for me, for us. You were even there for my dad. Your editing of this story helped make it even better. Thank you.

My acquisitions editor, Terry Whalin, from Morgan James Publishing, who believed in me, supported me, and stayed in contact with me all these years, encouraging me to write a book with them. I appreciate all you have done for me. Thank you.

Angie Kiesling, of The Editorial Attic, whose comments, suggestions, and changes helped make Dad's story more enjoyable. I was always grateful for your quick feedback. Thank you.

My mom, Carol, who has loved, supported me, and helped fill in the gaps of Dad's story. You have shown me such strength in the difficult times and loss of your husband, John. You have modeled for me how to live life fully, despite your circumstances. You love so passionately those around you. You are always thinking of other people and caring for their needs. You are incredibly thoughtful. I love spending time with you and am so thankful for you.

My girly girl, Shannon. You have filled my life with so much joy, excitement, purpose, and blessings. I enjoy every moment I spend with you. Lord willing, I can't wait to see all that God has for you. You have inspired me and many others. I love you with all my heart.

My wonderful husband, James, who allowed God to use him. Thank you for listening and acting on God's prompting. Thank you for being a man after God's heart. I have loved our journey together. Lord willing, I look forward to a lifetime of exploring, laughter, and love with you. Thank you for all your encouragement, support, and editing of Dad's story. You make life better. You make life sweeter. I love you.

Finally, and most importantly, thank You, God, for orchestrating this puzzle of Dad's life. I don't always understand everything at the time, but I trust You, Lord. I know that when You say no to my requests, it means You have something better for me. *"For my thoughts are not your thoughts, neither are your ways my ways, declares the Lord"* (Is. 55:8). Thank You for being a God who cares and loves. You are good!

The Layout

*Better to appear foolish than to open your mouth
and remove all doubt.*
Mark Twain

A Few Words First

People who don't remember history
are doomed to repeat it.
Chuckism

This is my personal story about my dad. He loved my two brothers and me the same, but each of us had a different relationship with him.

Charlie and Mike took over Dad's business and did an amazing job of growing it. They had business in common with Dad and enjoyed a different side of him. Dad was proud of them and loved all three of us very much. I have included some of my brothers' stories, but this is really my story of Dad. How I knew him.

Most importantly, we are all players in God's big plan, pieces in His big puzzle. Just as God orchestrated the individual personalities and messages of the Bible authors, so God used many people in Dad's life to reach him.

Looking back, it's amazing to see how it all unfolded. All the pieces came together. A puzzle can be a beautiful picture that is not fully seen until it is complete. It has many pieces that work together in different places at different times to make the magnificent picture complete and enable it to tell the story of the puzzle. We don't know why it takes so long and why it's so hard for some pieces of the puzzle to come into the story.

Sometimes we have to step back from the puzzle to get a glimpse of the bigger picture that is taking shape.

God knows the picture, and God alone receives the glory. He makes all things possible.

Words of Wisdom?

Fords pass Cadillacs all day long.
They just have to work harder.
Chuckism

Wedding Advice? Really?

You reap what you sow.
Chuckism

It was supposed to be the perfect night. God had clearly brought James and me together. For this special night we chose the Governor's Mansion, high on a hill overlooking breathtaking Santa Fe, New Mexico. Complete with a large white tent with string lights all around, crystal chandeliers hanging from the ceiling, and chair covers with big bows in the back. There to celebrate with us were 165 of our friends and family who had been beside us through our difficult journeys of pain and heartache over the last several years.

My dad was graciously flying my brothers and their wives to our big day on a chartered jet. He'd later take my mom, James, and me back to California so we could see local family and start our honeymoon driving up the coast to Washington. From there, we'd go on my dream cruise to Alaska.

We'd had a short engagement—in everyone else's eyes anyways—six weeks. Given that timeframe, I needed a dress off the rack! My fifteen-year-old daughter Shannon wanted us to fly to Kleinfeld Bridal in New York City, where the television show *Say Yes to the Dress* is filmed. Miraculously, I found one that didn't even need to be altered and was well under budget, which is unusual for me. The tight-fitting mermaid-style dress made me feel beautiful. I was excited for everyone to see it, especially James.

I hoped my dad would like it too. As we took photos before the wedding ceremony, I saw him coming toward me. I smiled even wider than I had been all day. I was so glad he had made it. He smiled his big grin, and I noticed one of his front teeth was missing. *Where's his tooth?* I wondered. I shrugged it off because at least he was there. Until that night, I wasn't confident he'd make it. I'd been checking in with my brothers regularly, hoping they would make sure Dad didn't back out.

Dad and I held each other as the photographer clicked away and created the pictures I knew I'd always cherish. Then it was time for me to go and get ready to walk down the aisle.

Before letting me go, Dad pulled me close to give me that last special father-daughter hug. As he held me tight, he leaned in close to my ear to share some last words of wisdom.

"Don't get fat," he said.

I guess that's not what I expected my father to say. But nothing would spoil this night. Not tonight.

That's my dad.

(2016) My wedding: Dad and Trish; photo by Frank Frost

The Inside Story

There is always a better way!
Chuckism

Destined to Be Different

*Better to live your life interesting and productive
than easy and comfortable.*
Tom Sorenson

Dad was destined to be different, it seems.

He was born just outside Chicago, Illinois. Both of his parents became alcoholics. His father took uppers in the morning to get out of bed and downers at night to go to sleep. Dad was a gifted athlete who received the All-Around High School Gymnastics Award for Illinois and the Midwest in A.A.U. (Amateur Athletic Union). He was offered many college athletic scholarships. However, his father, Charles W. King, said he would only pay for college if Dad went to Dartmouth, his alma mater. But Dartmouth only had a club gymnastics team. Dad succumbed to his father's pressure and attended Dartmouth. He competed for two years at the club level, but it was difficult to continue as an elite athlete, so he worked to receive both a Bachelor of Science and Master of Science in Mechanical Engineering from Dartmouth College. His college friends called him "Snitzy," but most people called him Chuck.

My dad also completed the US Army Critical Skills Program. That, in and of itself, was a significant achievement. Still, he managed to go AWOL (Absent Without Official Leave: a term used in the US Military to describe a soldier or other military member absent from their post but without intent to desert). He hopped a wall to get off the base and later talked his way back in. He was not a deserter.

After college and his time in the military, Dad ventured West in search of "the perfect burger." He'd tell you he ended up in Menlo Park, California, because of his love for the legendary Oasis burger. The "O," as it was called, was a popular burger hangout where you'd enter the dimly lit room and feel the crunch of peanut shells beneath your feet that everyone had dropped on the floor. Then you'd search for familiar names carved into the wooden tables.

Menlo Park was where he fell in love with my mother, Carol Argilla. Their marriage had a rough start when Dad's parents barged in on the wedding ceremony, spewing drunken obscenities about Carol. Luke (Carol's dad) escorted them out, and they remained on the outside throughout most of my parents' married life. This meant my mom got to spend time with her family who lived nearby and didn't need to divide her time going to Chicago to see his parents. It was difficult for my mom, knowing her husband's parents didn't accept her. Once Dad's mom passed away his father tried to make up for how they had treated Carol by giving her his wife's large diamond wedding ring. It was his way of offering peace.

A few years later, they were living in a tiny apartment with two children, and Mom really wanted to buy a house. Dad did not! He wanted to put all his money in the business. Mom won this battle, and it turned out to be an awesome investment. They bought their home, located next to an elementary school, for $33,000. Thirty years later it was worth $900,000. Now, they did have lawn furniture in their house for the longest time. Thankfully, Mom's father owned a garden-and-pet-supply store or they might have had only boxes to sit on because Dad didn't want to spend money on real furniture. As kids, we loved being next door to all the fields, tennis courts, and activity the school offered us. It was the perfect energy outlet for three young, athletic children. Way to go, Mom!

As a young newlywed, Dad embarked on a career in real estate development. Ultimately, he was involved in developing 135 industrial and office buildings, primarily in the San Francisco Bay Area. He also built in Southern California, Illinois, Ohio, South Carolina, Texas, Taiwan, and Thailand.

He created "The King Empire," as many people called it. He started in real estate development and expanded to Venture Capital. He had three main companies: SteriGenics, Records Retention, and King and Lyons. He was the cofounder, major shareholder, and chairman of the board of SteriGenics International, the world's largest-capacity gamma sterilizer of medical disposables and other products. They were on the cutting edge in the United States, irradiating spices and other foods. This improves the safety and extends the shelf life by reducing or eliminating microorganisms and insects. He was very excited when he took SteriGenics public.

He acquired a bankrupt record storage company and merged it with Filesafe Inc. to create the largest record storage company in Northern California. Thankfully, he sold the company right before the world went digital.

Finally, along with Bud Lyons, he merged King and Lyons, their real estate development company, with Security Capital, a REIT (Real Estate Investment Trust: a company that owns or finances income-producing real estate). Modeled after mutual funds, REITs provide investors with regular income streams.

Security Capital changed their name to Prologis, which is traded on the stock exchange and is very successful today.

You might guess he was the definition of a workaholic. Dad worked long hours at the office, only to come home and continue working from his bed. The "King genes" meant he almost always woke up in the middle of the night to get in a few more hours.

Despite his high profile as a developer and entrepreneur, Dad was a loner, intensely private, but happiest in the company of family and friends. To them, he is remembered for his kindness and generosity. Regardless of his stature in life, he treated everybody equally and with respect.

(1952) Gymnastics: parallel bars

(1953) Chuck in high school

(1961) Carol and Chuck's wedding

Chuckisms

*Dream, then go after that dream
with sweat and commitment.*
Chuckism

Dad loved inspirational quotes and proselytization, so I've used one at the beginning of each chapter. Those around him called them "Chuckisms." Some were exact quotes, but many were a variation of a quote. I kept the variation. For most of his life, up until 2008, he wrote his favorite sayings in his small daily pocket planner. We heard them so often that when he rattled off one of his quotes, we'd roll our eyes and say, "Number 101." Acting as if each saying had a number.

When I was in high school competing at the California State Track and Field Championships, Dad gave me a slip of paper on which he had typed out the saying, *"Dream, then go after that dream with sweat and commitment."* It became one of my favorite sayings. I might have rolled my eyes whenever he told me a Chuckism, but the truth is I always loved them and found them inspiring and motivating.

When Shannon was three, he took photos of her on a miniature red chair while talking to her in "Chuckisms" and pointing his finger at her to make sure she listened to his wisdom. He sent a photo collage to her with a note that said,

"Dearest Shannon, you are the only daughter of my only daughter. Life will offer you many choices. Today, you promised me that you will always make the smart choice, not the easy choice. You will always be in my heart. Love, Grandpa Charlie."

Remember, make the smart choice!

When grandpa speaks Shannon listens.

(2003) Grandpa telling Shannon "Chuckisms"

The Unusual Adventures

*It is better to celebrate life than
to celebrate achievements.*
Chuckism

Dad's life was filled with fascinating exploits. "Never short of dreaming up another adventure," as Dad often said. If there was a gold medal for the person who did unique, fascinating, and unusual experiences, I think my dad would have gotten it. He also loved including others and the thrill of watching them have their own first-time outrageous experience.

One snowy day in Chicago when Dad was young, he hooked his sled to the back of a car and then rode behind it as the car reached speeds of up to sixty miles per hour. This was an adrenaline high until his sled slammed into a parked car when he went around a turn. He was hospitalized for several days, lost a few teeth, and got seventy stitches on his face and inside his mouth.

When he was sixteen, his parents left town for a few days. While they were gone, Dad bought a car (The Rock), which resembled something Al Capone would have driven, for fifty dollars and painted it himself. Then someone vandalized it, and part of the car was found hanging in a tree.

One college summer break, he spent ten weeks on a motorcycle traveling through England, Europe, and North Africa.

He climbed the Matterhorn in Zermatt, Switzerland, and almost didn't survive because he didn't have the proper clothing, socks, and gloves. He had expected the weather to be good, and it turned out to be incredibly windy and cold.

In 1956, he worked on a ship out of Montreal, Canada, then sailed to Europe.

For a honeymoon gift, he gave Carol a backpack, sweatshirt, and sleeping bag. They spent five months hiking around the world, staying in youth hostels, camps, or at people's houses they met along the way. They had almost no money and their camera had a pinhole in it, so they ended up with no photos from the trip.

Dad was a pilot and owned an older Piper Comanche airplane (shared with four partners) that he purchased for $14,000. He made an emergency landing in a field in Oregon during a rainstorm and had to leave the plane for weeks because it was stuck in the mud and they couldn't get it out. His partners were not happy about this at all.

He sponsored a hot air balloon owned by Dan Newby and went ballooning in the Rockies—Colorado, Nevada, Utah, and California. When he took others up, or if you were part of the crew, it was always a spectacular show, complete with the first-flight champagne ceremony.

Getting up at 3 a.m. to help get the balloon ready for the Dawn Patrol or a contest was a mixture of exhaustion and exhilaration. The excitement of the team working together to take the balloon out of the bag. Then holding the opening as the whirl of the fan fills it with cold air. Next the pilot sends several blasts from the burners and the balloon begins to stand upright. Seeing the picture on the custom balloon come to life in its full glory. Knowing hands down we had the best balloon in the show. A first of its kind, called *Beach Ball*. It was brighter than all the other balloons and the colors of the rainbow. There were dolphins, sand buckets, shovels, and beach balls.

The ground crew put their weight on the side of the basket to keep the balloon from floating away and waited for the signal to launch. Finally, with a loud whistle from the Zebra (launch director), it was our turn for take-off. The crew took their weight off the basket, and with several steady bursts of heat, it lifted off the ground to the cheers of the crowd.

The ultimate thrill was being in the basket and waving to all those on the ground clapping and screaming. Then we were heading up in the air in the balloon surrounded by all the beautiful colors. The quiet of the sky was mixed with the loud whooshing noise, the surging power and the heat of the gas that kept *Beach Ball* in the air. Looking down, you could see the ground racing quickly below you; at other times you just seemed to float in one place.

Then there was being in the balloon chase crew. You never knew what you were in for. We'd follow the balloon as it flew over hills and valleys or into fenced-in fields filled with pesky bramble bushes. One time, they even landed awkwardly in the city dump of Snowmass, Colorado. Chuckles, as my dad's pilot Dan called him, preferred the thrill of winning the competitions, and one time in Reno he won a Honda Civic in a key grab.

In 1984 Dad and Dan competed in the famous Gordon Bennet Balloon race, which is the world's oldest gas balloon race and "regarded as the premier event of world balloon racing," according to the *Los Angeles Times*. The aim of the contest is simple: to fly the farthest distance from the launch site. They hoped to go a thousand miles.

Dad spent weeks preparing excitedly. He built it up to be this incredible multi-day expedition and even bought special gear that weighed very little but would keep him warm at high altitude.

The race began and the balloon ascended . . . but suddenly they realized they were having equipment failure. There was an opening in the balloon top. Panic seized them as they started throwing everything they could overboard in hopes of going farther. Disappointingly they were forced down. Their big adventure was a catastrophe, essentially, as they took off, went up, and almost immediately came back down. Dad didn't often finish last. Ouch!

Dan insisted, "Neither one of us ever chose to 'grow up'; we refused to capitulate to aging."

Dad once flew a date from San Francisco to Los Angeles in a chartered jet for dinner on the Goodyear Blimp while flying over the city. He got a lot of creativity points for that one.

He whitewater rafted the Colorado River, which was thrilling and gave a different perspective of the Grand Canyon with the rugged canyon walls all around.

He rode a helicopter into the rainforest of Kauai and hiked for miles, enjoying the waterfalls and the adrenalin rush of cliff jumping into a swimming hole.

He even had me join him for a three-day race car driving class at Bob Bondurant School of High Performance Driving at Sears Point International Raceway near Sonoma, California. A side note: I did beat Dad and his friends in the competition driving the race course on the last day! Later, the training saved my life in a torrential downpour on a California freeway. I knew how to respond when the person in front of me was spinning out of control.

He bought a forty-foot sailboat and sailed under the picturesque Golden Gate Bridge in San Francisco. To our dismay, he had crammed for the sailing test. This didn't give any of us a lot of confidence. Fortunately, sailing didn't last long as he wisely decided it wasn't very safe for him.

Needing a new challenge, Dad started helicopter pilot lessons only to realize that it was incredibly difficult to work the rotary. It was a smart move when he discontinued this pursuit.

I always thought it was so cool when just the two of us went on an overnight camping trip on his Honda 250cc or 550cc motorcycle. We went off on our adventure, with me clinging on to his waist for dear life. With all we needed on the back of the bike, we'd head to the campground, which I was sure was hours away from home. Years later, I found out we barely went twenty minutes away. One of the best parts was that I got to pick the menu for dinner. Typically, hot dogs, M&M's, and s'mores. This was the beginning of my motorcycle days. Years later, I graduated to riding my own Harley Davidson motorcycle (so did he!).

He rode his Harley-Davidson motorcycle to the Sturgis Motorcycle Rally in South Dakota and even went to the legendary fiftieth anniversary in 1990. Half a million crazy bikers take over the city of Sturgis each year. Once, with his three children and friends, we stayed in a forty-foot RV at the Buffalo Chip Campground. The campground came alive at night, and rock bands played until 2 a.m. People dressed in the craziest biker clothes (this made for great people watching) and partied all night long (while we were trying to sleep). My then-husband Pat and I were part of many of these fun adventures. One time, along with Dad, we continued our ride north to Canada. We visited Lake Louise, Banff, and then went across to the province of Victoria. From Vancouver, Dad flew home, and

I rode his huge full-dresser Harley motorcycle down through Oregon and ended at Dad's house south of San Francisco, a 3,500-mile trip.

His big "failure"? He went skydiving and broke his femur bone in his leg and sprained his other ankle on his first jump upon landing. He had to be in a wheelchair for several weeks. I was ruthless and saw it as my opportunity to tease him, and he'd retaliate by throwing his crutch at me.

His favorite splurge was to charter a jet for snow skiing in Colorado or other adventures. Flying in a private jet was a wonderful, extravagant, lavishly decadent experience. One minute before the flight left, you drove straight up to the plane, handed them your luggage, walked up the red carpet, and sat down in a plush leather seat. Once in the air, you ate things like shrimp cocktail, yummy cookies, or fresh fruit, along with whatever drinks you wished to have. There was a snack drawer filled with everything you shouldn't eat. We would typically stuff our purses with the variety of cookies, nuts, and candies. No, it wasn't stealing. It came with the flight. It was the best!

Once he splurged and took several family members in a stretch limo from the Denver airport to Beaver Creek. His justification was that it was the same price as the shuttle van. He organized a group snowmobiling day and maneuvered the back woods and flew across the open spaces surrounded by the Colorado Rockies.

There was also the Five Star Enchantment Resort nestled in the vibrant-hued rock formations of Boynton Canyon in Sedona, Arizona. As a rule, he only went on a full moon and preferred the sky aglow with the huge harvest full moon. He wanted the experience to be perfect and spectacular for whomever he brought.

Dad wanted to go on the Orient Express, an international passenger train in Europe and a showcase of luxury and comfort. His purpose was to visit his longtime friend "Piano Man" Micky Poage, who played at Micky's Piano Bar in Vail, Colorado. Micky had been employed to play the piano on the Orient Express, but there were three different trains, and he didn't know on which train he was going to play. Dad took the risk and booked the trip, which happened to be on the right train, making a wonderful experience even more unique. As Micky was playing, he introduced everyone to his good friend Chuck, who had come to see him play.

He and Debe had a tea party for the three granddaughters: Lauren, Grace, and Shannon. They hired actors to dress as Alice in Wonderland and the Mad Hatter. The tea party was a real hit, complete with jewels, feather boas, cookie decorating, nail painting, and tea (okay, lemonade). Dad needed to wear a tuxedo jacket, but it was too small. When he put it on, it ripped in half down the back. Then he duct taped it together and wore it proudly. Duct tape fixes everything.

For the grandsons, Grandpa dressed up as Spider Man and hosted a Spider-Man-themed sleep over. On another occasion, he took them for a private karate lesson.

Dad got a natural high from the "wow effect." He loved seeing the excitement upon the faces of those he took on these incredible ventures. If you were privy to joining him on one, you got to see him in action and in his element. He loved outrageous experiences and sharing them with those he loved!

First car, "The Rock"

Hot air balloon: *Beach Ball*

Honda camping trip: Dad and Trish

(1993) Harley trip to Sturgis, SD

Dad's friends: McClellans, Daltons, Newby, and Navone

(1998) Snowmobiling in Colorado

(2006) Mad Hatter tea party: Lauren, Grace, and Shannon

Dad duct taped his jacket

The King Character

*Truth doesn't change or go away,
no matter how far you run.*
Chuckism

Dad was unique and a character that everyone loved. He had his quirks, but we all do. He gave me many opportunities in life and exposed me to a variety of things. He wanted me to have culture, learn about the arts, and be able to talk about current affairs and politics. He believed in higher education and especially at an Ivy League school. He always encouraged his kids and grandchildren to go back East to school. Not that we did!

The King Kids

When Dad put his mind to something, failure was not an option.

Obviously, this was true with his businesses, but it was also true with just about whatever he did. This included raising his three kids, Trish (eldest), Charlie, and Mike (youngest who looks like Dad). He thought we turned out pretty well. (Mom gets a lot of credit too!)

When they were younger, Charlie and Mike were exceptional athletes. Charlie excelled in football, track, and baseball. He was and still is one of the prettiest skiers on the mountain. When he was younger, he'd be vadeling down the moguls, go off one, do a helicopter (360-degree turn), land, and effortlessly continue on his way down the run.

Mike excelled in football, soccer, and track and placed in the NCAA Division 1 Championships in the 400-meter hurdles in college. He still holds the record at Menlo Atherton High School in the hurdles. He, too, is a beautiful skier.

My talented brothers gave me the incentive and drive to compete with them. In fact, when I was young, all I wanted to do was beat them, especially in sports.

Dad and Mom taught my brothers and me to ski at a young age by putting a rope around our waist. Mom would be in front, I'd be in the middle, with Dad behind me, and we'd go down the mountain. It worked great. Now you can buy harnesses to do the same thing. Once we knew how to ski, he loved leading the way down the run. He'd click his poles together behind him saying "follow me," and we all did. Then he'd tell you to hold your poles in front of you like you're holding a tray. Every morning we had to go pick up the groomed run report at the ticket office. There was no internet back then to supply the information.

When we were little we'd go skiing at Lake Tahoe. We parked the car what seemed to be a mile away. Okay, not quite, but it felt like it to a seven-year-old. He made us carry our skis and poles while stomping uphill in our ski boots to the base of the mountain. We'd be whining, weak from the weight of the equipment, and in tears. Dad wanted to build character and make us tough by having us carry our own skis. He always wanted us to be tough!

Then while we were on the mountain he was all about the "vertical feet"—as many runs as we could do to maximize the value of the ticket. The more runs, the better the value. However, what was not built into the equation was the weather.

If it was freezing, snowy, or windy, he wouldn't let us end our day. We'd be miserable and want to stop. Maybe we got a quick hot chocolate break, but remember, we needed to get our money's worth. Get those vertical feet in.

Dad taught me to swim at a young age by putting a belt around my waist with a Styrofoam float attached to the back. Each time I swam he cut out a chunk of the Styrofoam. Eventually, he just threw me in the water with only the belt on my waist. He definitely didn't coddle me.

As the eldest child and only daughter, I was "Daddy's girl." Okay, really, I was a tomboy. Sometimes I'd hear Dad say I was his "project." He taught me various sports to see how good I could be. This was just before and at the beginning of Title IX, a federal regulation which states that no one in scholastic programs will be discriminated against based upon their sex. This translated to equal opportunities at schools for men and women and resulted in more girls joining sports.

In the backyard, Dad taught me back handsprings and spotted me on back flips on the trampoline. He taught me how to throw a football and a baseball. This led to me being the first girl in Little League Baseball in Northern California. Here is where trying to keep up with my brothers paid off. Dad almost took the league to court to gain the right for girls to play, resulting in me playing first base for the McDonald's Major Little League team. He believed in me and fought for me when he felt it was worth it.

I had Dad's athletic skills and drive and could play most any sport. I was NorCal Athlete of the Year in 1980 for three sports at Menlo Atherton High School in California: diving/ swimming, soccer (goalie), and track and field (high jump, long jump, hurdles, wherever they needed me). I even did a men's decathlon in high school. I was inducted into the San Mateo County Hall of Fame and Menlo Atherton High School Hall of Fame for three sports.

I made the 1988 U.S. Olympic Team in the high jump and then took eleven years off and had two children. Eventually, I returned to competition and became the multiple world record holder for women aged forty to forty-four, twelve-time USA Masters Champion, and World Masters Champion . . . but that's another story.

My dad and mom (also very athletic) gave me great genes. With all that said, I recognize my abilities are a gift from God. I can do nothing apart from Him.

I'm incredibly proud of and grateful for my brothers, who eventually took the helm of Dad's business, made solid business choices, and brought it to a whole new level. Both men are philanthropic and care about others. I know Dad was proud of them. Gratefully, we all share a faith in Christ. Both brothers married wonderful women and are engaged with their families, always making them a priority.

An Exceptional Athlete

When Dad was younger, he was game for just about any activity or sport and was good at whatever he did. He was the High School State Gymnastic Champion and captain of his team. Dad was the only competitor for the Dartmouth Club in the championship division of the New England A.A.U. gymnastics meet. He accumulated enough points to place the college third in the team totals.

He loved playing tennis, and we'd play together as a family. When he water skied, he'd show off with a thumbs-up, trying to get the driver to go faster. He always liked a good photo.

Snow skiing was his favorite. He was a beautiful skier, fluid and smooth, and he loved his groomed runs! For years and years he wore the same super-ugly jacket and bandana until we finally bought him new ones.

He loved to throw the football, baseball, and jump on the trampoline in the backyard. He bought us a wobble board because he knew it was good for our coordination, and we'd take turns timing ourselves to see who could stay on the longest.

Dad's close friend and accountant, Tom Sorenson, once told me about being at Enchantment Resort with Dad and three couples: the Daltons, Navones, and Sorensons. They had a "tournament" croquet course. They all ganged up on Chuck, sacrificing their own chances to win in an attempt to bring him down—but he still won!

Apparently, there were only two things he couldn't do: skydiving and scuba diving because while under water he was paralyzed by claustrophobia.

Above all, Dad was competitive, focused, and good at whatever sport he did. He wanted to win. (Wonder where I got that attitude from? Hmm . . .)

"King Standard Time"

Dad was always late, and I'm not talking five minutes. I grew up on what we called "King Standard Time," which was at least one to two hours late.

My brothers and I remember running through airports trying to catch flights, only to have the airplanes' doors close on us. We'd pound on the door, hoping they'd open. For the record, a few times he talked his way in. Definitely a different time than today. One time, Dad missed his flight. To kill time, he sat at the bar and then missed his next flight too. That made for a long day.

Once in college, I was competing at a track meet at Berkeley. I told Dad, "You have to get there right on time. If you are one minute late, you'll miss me." He drove for an hour and still missed the race.

Another time, my son, Connor, was competing all day at the USA National Fencing Championships in San Jose, California, just twenty-five minutes from Dad's home. Dad showed up only to find that Connor was finished. How could he miss it all? He didn't account for the time spent when he hit a pole in the parking lot with his car. Thankfully, no one was hurt. However, we got a great photo of Dad, Connor, and me at the championships.

Didn't Appreciate Daily Routine

In the early years, Dad didn't appreciate daily routine and small talk. This was a result of liking the "big stuff." Therefore, when we'd talk, if I didn't have anything big and exciting to talk about, the conversation was incredibly short, just a few minutes. He'd say, "Well, I don't have anything more to say."

However, life isn't always about national championships and outrageous events. Life is made up of lots of little moments, and it's about living each moment to the fullest. But Dad didn't embrace this philosophy.

Trusted People

Dad lived his life by "I trust my fellow man!" It's how he justified leaving his keys on the floor of his car with the door unlocked. One year, he got his little Datsun 240z stolen three times. Once it was found in a ditch all stripped. Another time somebody stole it the night before we left for Tahoe for Christmas, and it had all our Christmas presents in it. That was really sad for us kids.

Thankfully, for the most part, he surrounded himself with amazing partners and people who were incredibly trustworthy. However, there was one exception. It rocked his world when one of his best friends, who was his attorney and partner in a few projects, embezzled a lot of money from him.

Since Dad believed in people and was very loyal, he didn't see this coming. He told Tom, "He can't steal from me because he's my attorney!" Tom "nearly fell over laughing." He didn't treat people this way, and he took it especially hard because they were friends. Justifiably so! Dad was not able to laugh about this incident, but he did have a sense of humor. An odd one though.

(2005) Dad's seventieth birthday: Charlie, Trish, and Mike

(2008) Like father, like son: Mike and Dad

Dad spotting Trish doing back handsprings

Water skiing

(2008) U.S. National Fencing Championships:
Trish and Connor - photo by Amy Alden

Just for Grins

A Sense of Humor

Growing up, Dad loved starting out his day blasting the music to "Zip-a-Dee-Doo-Dah." He'd go on and on, "Zip-a-dee-ay, my, oh my, what a wonderful day . . ." while he sang, danced, and jumped up clicking his heels together in the air.

One of his favorite and most amusing projects was when the real estate market was super weak in the early 1990s. He had a friend take a photo of him looking like a homeless man with a dirty face, wearing tattered clothes and Birkenstocks and lying on a park bench with a sign that read: "Real Estate Developer. Will Work for Legal Fees." He gave this to his business friends and hung a large photo of it proudly in his home.

He bought nice T-shirts for his two secretaries and myself (the girls in his life) that said "Charlie's Angels" when the television show came out.

One Thanksgiving when I was in high school, Dad looked for something special to do with his three kids for the holiday. The best thing he could come up with was taking us to the horse races to get turkey dogs. Okay, they were just plain hot dogs. He gave each of us twenty dollars, and whoever came back with the most money after betting on the horse races got twenty dollars more. I typically pocketed ten dollars and gambled the other ten. That way I always went home with some money. Obviously I was not a big risk taker.

At Christmas, he'd take us and our friends to ski in Vail, Colorado, without ever arranging for a place to stay. Remember, this was Christmas. He called it an adventure. We called it stressful! We'd show up at the Vail Lodge with no room, and he'd beg and plead for a place to stay. At least we had a warm lobby to sit in and hot chocolate or apple cider to drink while he negotiated.

He did lots of silly things with the grandchildren. When he was learning computer graphics, he took a photo of himself with his grandson Timothy. He morphed himself into a tough biker dude complete with black nail polish. Timothy appeared as Bamm-Bamm Rubble, the cartoon character from the cartoon series *The Flintstones*.

He sent my son, Connor, chocolate-covered "Bear Poop" with a note: *Connor, I walked all over the mountain looking for the best Bear Poos for you. Taste these poos. Then call me and tell me if I did a good job finding the best poos. Love you, Grandpa Charlie.*

We never knew what would happen, and still don't know what happened, when the grandchildren spent the night at Grandpa and Grandma's. Frankly, we parents were always concerned. They usually stayed up most of the night and were filled with ice cream, candy, and all things junk, including raiding the endless candy drawer. It was a real treat, pun intended, for them to stay there, but it did mean the parents were left dealing with cranky kids the next day.

When they remodeled the condo, they put a tiny room in the wall that was covered by a picture board so you didn't know it was there. It was a "secret hiding place where no parents were allowed to go." The kids had to climb a ladder and then crawl inside, and it was magical. Grandma Debe painted a castle on the wall with glow-in-the-dark paint that only lit up when the lights were off. Other paintings and mirrors adorned the walls, and an adult could never stand up in it because the ceiling was so low. It was filled with dress-up outfits to your heart's delight. Which princess were you going to be today? There were fun high-heeled shoes, purses, jewelry, wigs, hats, superhero outfits, toys, and more. It was every child's dream. The granddaughters always put on a fashion show for Grandpa, and they got to dress up Grandma too. What sweet memories!

Grandpa knew Connor, my son, was motivated by money. One overnight with Connor wearing his camo footy pajamas (most likely in the middle of the day), he offered him five dollars to eat an actual bug. Connor, like Grandpa, was always up for a challenge where there was the possibility of financial gain. Of course, Connor ate the bug! Grandpa sent a photo to him of the funny remembrance with a note saying, "*I hope you are not what you eat! Love, Grandpa Charlie.*"

His favorite motivational book was *The Little Engine That Could,* and when he read it to my children, they all wore train engineers' hats. He wanted the grandchildren to have the mindset "I think I can. I think I can. I think I can." That was important to him.

Incidentally, and paradoxically perhaps, his favorite Chuckism to me was, "Do as I say, not as I do!"

All about a Good Story

Dad was all about a good story. Most of his "good stories" were comprised of his infamous adventures, but there were others he loved to tell.

Once he took my cousin Deborah on her first balloon ride. Without the pilot, we were alone in the balloon, which was tethered to the bumper of the car. Suddenly, the rope came loose from the car, and we started floating away. My brother Charlie realized what was happening and jumped up to grab the basket. In our eyes he was the superhero that saved the day! He was hanging on for dear life, his legs dangling in the air, as we floated thirty feet up into the sky toward some ominous power lines.

Most parents would freak out seeing their kids in a runaway balloon. Not my dad. He thought this was a great photo opportunity and crouched down to get the perfect shot. He was always trying for the "perfect photo," which was often rather annoying. In this case, I'll admit it was a great picture.

Surprisingly, I'd been listening to the pilot when he gave his safety talk and mentioned, "If you want to come down, you just pull this rope and it opens the flap in the top of the balloon and lets the hot air out." My dad told the story of the balloon adventure (mishap) for the rest of his life. Like I said, he was all about the story!

When Dad was newly married, we were at my cousin's wedding. He and Debe were laughing hysterically and proceeded to tell everyone at their table how earlier he had taken a Viagra pill. He couldn't find his hearing aid battery. When he laid out the contents of his pocket on the table, there was the blue pill. He realized he had swallowed the hearing aid battery thinking it was the Viagra pill. A new favorite story for his collection.

Micky, "The Piano Man," said he will always remember Chuck for his "quirky wit and sense of humor—what a LAUGH he had." His favorite funny story that Dad told him was when Dad threw away his cell phone with his drive-through McDonald's burger trash! Surprising, since Dad hardly ever used a cell phone.

In 2015, the Silicon Valley Humane Society hosted a fundraiser called "The Fur Ball." It was a formal event, where even your dogs dressed up. Dad and Debe thought this would make the best story and invited us, along with all the other grandchildren, their families, and dogs. Shannon and I planned for a year. We ordered a purple dress for Lola (our rescue Yorkie) and a black tuxedo for Theo (our Yorkipoo) and put hundreds of crystals on them. This was going to be quite the family experience. Unfortunately, Dad and Debe got sick and didn't go, so we just took photos with them before we left. My brothers, Shannon, and her cousins Evan and Lauren all attended this amazing evening that raised almost one million dollars.

Dad loved sharing a story with those who'd listen, and we treasure the memories and laughs they all created.

(1993) "Zip-A-Dee-Doo-Dah" heel click: Deborah Tucker

"Will work for legal fees"

Trish in Charlie's Angels shirt

Grandpa and Timothy computer morphed

(2007) Connor "I ate a bug club"

(2003) Reading to Connor in engineers' hats

(1989) Balloon floating away

(1996) Viagra/battery story: Debe, Dad, and Trish

Dad's Treasure

Big mistake if you think a rich external life will lead to a rich internal life.
Chuckism

Wasn't about Things

One of Dad's favorite sayings was, "He who dies with the most toys wins." But in actuality, he had very few toys—only his six-foot plaster butler, his 1986 Porsche 928, and an heirloom grandfather clock. For years, every time he drove the 928 he had to put steering wheel fluid in it. He always drove with a full gas can behind the driver's seat because he ran out of gas so often. He thought he was being prepared. I think he was being careless.

He was not a big spender. Things didn't matter to him, and he wasn't ruled by his things. They were not what he treasured.

He wasn't flashy, and frankly you'd never know he was rich by looking at him or talking to him. He always wore saggy Levi's blue jeans, worn cowboy boots, and a polo shirt. He had crisp white hair and could have been a stand-in for talk show host Phil Donahue. If he had an important meeting or needed to go to the bank to borrow money, he might add a sport coat. He wore blue most of the time and occasionally white, gray, or black. He didn't even own a nice watch. Before he'd consider replacing his cowboy boots, he'd have them resoled.

As he grew older, the boots were hidden away beneath the hanging clothes in the back of his closet and he only wore slippers. He claimed his toes hurt from all the times he broke them during his years doing gymnastics. He even wore slippers to his stepdaughter's wedding in Las Vegas and to his grandson Evan's high school playoff football game on a cold, rainy night.

Generous

Dad was generous to his family and friends. He believed in his kids, and if we needed support for a philanthropic cause, he came through. He was always willing to take our friends on whatever adventure we were going on and treated them like family. (I admit once that meant they had the privilege of cleaning out and dumping the RV sewer tank.) He also gave to various foundations and charities.

He included many of his friends, my brothers, Debe's family, my girlfriends, and even their husbands in private chartered jet trips. Sometimes there were so many of us they'd send a Gulfstream G4, as seen on *Criminal Minds* (the TV series), flying the team to their investigation. It was always an amazing experience. You never wanted to fly commercial again!

I remember Dad telling about his niece Deborah Tucker, at the age of twenty-one, moved to Los Angeles to become an actress. It was a bold move, and she had been close to getting the role on several auditions. Finally, she asked the casting director why she didn't get it. He said her teeth were too gray. When she called my dad and mentioned it to him, he promptly responded by paying to have her teeth whitened. She got a leading role in the television series *Living Dolls*, starring Halle Berry. Way to go, Dad and Deborah!

A funny side note: when Deborah was born, she was named after the actress Deborah Lynn. Dad said to his sister, "What is she going to be? A movie star when she grows up?" Little did he know that's exactly what God had in mind for her.

He was super excited when he sent his two secretaries, Deborah and myself, to get our color charts done. They determine what season you are and decide which clothes suit your skin tone by choosing the right colors for your complexion, hair, and eye color. They made a little wallet with color swatches in it for us to make shopping easy. Then he bought Deborah and me clothes and makeup for college that were our "best colors." We felt like we were looking good!

For many years, he bought the airline tickets for the annual cancer foundation fundraiser.

Eight months before the Olympics, I needed some help. I was working between thirty and sixty hours a week, but I wasn't making much money. I had some new expenses for my training: coaches, regular chiropractic care, and massage. I was training for the heptathlon, seven events in track and field held over two days. Dad agreed to give me three hundred dollars a month so I could "get on with my life!" My mom also helped me each month. Together they were a big part of why I made the Olympic team in the high jump. I felt responsible for working even harder since they were supporting me. I could not have done it without them.

When I competed at the Olympics in Seoul, South Korea, Dad was there. Plus, he paid for airline tickets, housing in the Olympic Family Village, event tickets, and expenses for my entire family. Mom, my brothers, and my mother's parents (my grandparents) all watched me compete in the Olympic stadium—a once-in-a-lifetime experience that very few people ever have. It was a bonus for me to have my entire family in the stands cheering me on.

Dad treasured his family and friends. He was always generous with me, my brothers, and grandchildren, for which we are forever appreciative and thankful!

The Rush of the Deal

He loved the adrenalin rush of the deal. This is what motivated him. The challenge, the thrill of the risk, making things happen. He wasn't interested in the money for its own sake. He liked the excitement of the businesses he created and the many beautiful buildings he built.

Dad liked the high from the deal, but not always. Tom Sorenson said, "He would sometimes get so nervous that he would start chewing a hangnail and rip it to the second knuckle! We would sit in his office drinking espresso and get so wired that we would both talk very fast and at the same time—driving everyone else in the office crazy."

Dad may have been nervous at times, but he made lots of phenomenal business decisions. In the process, he affected many lives in a positive way. Tom fondly states, "I don't have enough fingers and toes to count the people who owe their careers and their successes to Chuck—starting with several partners, but also contractors, architects, attorneys, and accountants—including me!" This was a huge part of his legacy.

A Lofty Goal

Dad had retired from the real estate business and as a venture capitalist and decided to concentrate on investing. This was a different world, and one he wasn't as familiar with. As always, he dove in feet first and learned all he could. Soon he felt he was an expert (which frankly was a problem), and with confidence and enthusiasm for the high of the deal, he began his investment journey. For a time, he was incredibly successful.

In 2006, Dad could see and taste it. He wasn't Bill Gates or Mark Zuckerberg, but he was well on his way to reaching his goal of being a billionaire. He liked the challenge. He had amassed a fortune, acquiring several buildings in one of the most expensive areas in the country, taking one company public and selling three businesses to large, successful companies.

With the creation of the King Empire and now his success in the investment world, he sadly developed a "God complex" when it came to making money. He felt invincible, like he could never lose his money because, according to him, with finger pointed, "I have more money than God. If I lost half of my money, which would never happen, I'd still be rich."

How much was enough? He always wanted more. He was rarely fulfilled with what he had already made and achieved. Little did he know the power in two simple words–content and satisfied.

The Tuckers and Kings skiing Vail

(1988) Olympic Games Seoul, Korea: family

Christine and Tom Sorenson

The Power of Words

The tongue is a small part of the body, but it can cause great havoc.
Chuckism

Keep It Brief

Dad answered his phone, "King here." His answering machine said, "King not here. Speak at the beep!" Referring to my guy friends, Dad advised me, "Don't talk his ears off." He wanted things written with a short summary. He was fearful of public speaking and wouldn't even give a toast at my wedding. This section needs to be brief because that's how he'd like it!

Loved Talking Business

Business conversations, however, were not brief. Dad lived and breathed business. It was all he wanted to talk about. He'd look at me and say, "I need to make a Money Call." At gatherings, he dragged people off into a corner to discuss business—partly because he didn't like big gatherings.

Occasionally, while driving to meetings in San Francisco or the East Bay, Tom and Dad talked so intensely they drove miles past their turnoff before they realized where they were. Once, Dad and Bob Schaberg visited Tom in Arizona. After leaving the airport, they drove over an hour in the wrong direction before realizing their mistake. They'd been talking business.

Jim, his roommate at Dartmouth, recalls the time in 1965 when Dad was tired and bored with engineering and then his brief stint selling homes. He wanted to pursue a career in industrial real estate and asked Jim if he knew any "Hot Shots" in the field who could give him some advice. Jim had a tennis partner who fit this description.

Dad wanted to impress them, so for their first meeting, he flew them to lunch at the Nut Tree in Vacaville, California, usually a quick thirty-minute flight away. After an hour in the air, one of the businessmen realized they were flying through fog and suggested they should be close to Vacaville where there is no fog in the summer. My dad quickly called San Francisco Control, which finally spotted them on the radar and informed them that they were many miles off course. The businessman whispered to Jim, "Does Charlie really know how to fly?" Dad had become so focused on the conversation he paid no attention to his instruments. Needless to say, the "Hot Shot" businessman was most impressed with Dad's skill sets and enthusiasm and invited Dad to join them in their operations. This was the beginning of his successful industrial real estate endeavors.

Critical of His Women

Dad liked his women thin, blonde, and quiet. He didn't like it when women talked a lot. Especially me or his wife. He often said I talked too much. Debe colored her hair blonde to "please her man." One time, right after the Olympics, I went out to the opera with two older men and my girlfriend Denise. I came down the stairs in high heels, my hair curled, wearing a dress and makeup (rare for me). Dad came up to me, pointed his finger at my face, and said, "Your eyebrows aren't dark enough." I didn't even know I should darken my eyebrows. That was the tomboy in me.

When I came home from college, I'd gained more weight than the "freshman fifteen." Dad filled up a backpack with books, threw it at me, and said, "Here, jump with this." Ouch!

The year before the Olympics, he asked me, "When are you going to move on with your life and get a real job?" In this case, it was a good thing I didn't listen to him!

At my wedding, he whispered in my ear, "Don't get fat." I definitely preferred Chuckisms to that statement. Some things never change.

(2001) Another day at the office: Connor and Shannon

A Life Change

*You have to get past blame before you
can move toward solutions.*
Chuckism

When I was fifteen, my dad and mom went on a vacation
to Tahiti. When they arrived home, they asked me and
my two brothers, Charlie (thirteen) and Mike (ten), to sit down
in the living room because they had something to tell us. "We
are getting a divorce," they said. Their cool vacation had been a
last-ditch effort to save the marriage. I guess it hadn't gone too
well. Dad packed his silver 911 Porsche with all his possessions
(which wasn't much) and drove up the road to stay in a condo
with a business friend.

This was a big life change. He began the next phase of his
life and slowly started becoming more of a hermit. Dad's friend
decided to sell the condo, but Dad didn't want to move out, so
he bought it. His small condo overlooked a golf course in
Menlo Park, California. But he didn't golf. He didn't even like
golf because he'd been scarred by a girlfriend in high school
who beat him badly in his first (and last) attempt at the game.
At the time he was a jock, a high school state champion in
gymnastics and an all-around athlete. He carried that loss with
him through life like one would carry ten extra pounds on their

waist. Anytime someone asked him about golf, he'd recount that story shamefully.

Living on a golf course sounds extravagant, but it really wasn't. For years, his condo had no furniture except his bed, office desk, office chair, kitchen table, and chairs. There was no cozy couch in the living room, just a cold tile floor on which you could do ballet twirls.

Then he moved his office into his bedroom. This was not a good idea for a sleep-deprived workaholic. He sat on his "throne" (a worn-out swivel chair) at his office desk making "Money Calls."

He could go days without leaving his condo. He'd seldom breathe fresh air except when walking down the driveway in his white baggy underwear and black mid-calf saggy socks to pick up his cherished *Wall Street Journal.* Often in the middle of the night, his fax machine beeped as it received messages from people in other parts of the world, who had no idea they were faxing a bedroom.

However, Dad had what he thought was a great idea for the kitchen wall of the condo. He had an accomplished artist from Palo Alto paint men floating in the air with buckets on their heads. Each man carried Dad's favorite foods on a tray: burgers, Diet Coke, ice cream, and M&M's. For a funny twist, he painted two realistic M&M's on the floor. It was very entertaining watching our friends struggle to pick them up.

There was also the six-foot plaster butler by the front door. Often, he offered some form of candy on his platter or the occasional Moose Poop.

The condo was practically on top of the San Andreas fault in Menlo Park. I remember one day when I was on the third level, the floor began to rumble, rock, and roll. As I'd been trained since I was a child, I immediately went to the doorway and watched Dad's chandelier sway from the door to the other edge of the wall and back again. Dad was in his doorway below. Trembling, I yelled, "We are going to die." Dad, distressed, shouted, "We are going to be broke." I was worried for our lives, and Dad was concerned about one of his buildings under construction. I learned that there were walls leaning against temporary supports. The building was also uninsured (earthquake insurance is too expensive in the Bay Area).

It turned out the earthquake was a 6.9 magnitude that shook the entire San Francisco Bay area. Thankfully, we lived, and the walls remained standing.

After the divorce, Dad started taking us skiing in Colorado during Christmas break. Following a day of skiing, we'd often spend our evenings at Micky's iconic piano bar in The Lodge at Vail. We drank hot chocolate, listened to Micky play and sing, and then Dad gave me money to put in his tip jar. Not the typical thing to do with your teenagers.

Eating Habits

His eating habits were terrible. You thought this if you were a nutritionist, a health-conscious person, or just breathing. As a single guy, he didn't eat like a King. It wasn't that he preferred Burger King, he was actually a McDonald's guy. Preferably their McRib. His freezer was full of ice cream as his refrigerator was bare. His food of choice was Häagen-Dazs ice cream. Needing an evening fix, he'd take us to the store to get a few pints. On our way home, he'd tear open the container with his teeth and wind it down to the bottom until the ice cream was gone, using only his mouth. If he was alone, my brother Mike occasionally spotted him driving his car while squeezing the entire pint of

Häagen-Dazs ice cream with his hands. As the ice cream oozed up out of the carton, his mouth engulfed it. No mess. No wasted time.

When Connor came to visit, they ate ice cream and cereal for breakfast. Dad had a huge candy drawer that was constantly filled with every kind of candy imaginable. He'd drink quarts of orange juice or lemonade and coffee with sugar-free hot chocolate and four to five artificial sweeteners per cup. A sweet junkie at his finest.

I'm not sure he knew what a vegetable tasted like. He searched the world for the "perfect burger," which had to be rare, and he ate more than his share of frozen microwavable dinners.

We'd think maybe if he got married he'd eat better. You are what you eat.

(1997) Wall Street Journal: Dad and Connor

The condo wall mural

The butler

Check Mate

The solution to a good marriage.
Keep your eyes open before marriage and
half open after marriage.
Chuckism

Hard to Pin Down

We never thought Dad would remarry. Many women tried, but he would never commit. He'd been divorced for almost twenty years and was dating Deborah, twenty years younger than him. She was beautiful, with long brown hair and blazing blue eyes. Debe was as sweet as could be and catered to his every whim. She had a figure that was a thirteen on a scale from one to ten, and as Dad said, "She looked great in jeans!" Which he'd proudly tell you was one of his requirements for a girlfriend!

Debe started talking about moving back to Iowa where her family lived because she couldn't afford to stay in the Bay Area. She stood firm and would not live with my dad unmarried. A good principle, but also an excellent strategy. Just like in chess, the King has been captured. Check mate, on her part.

Dad didn't want her to go. One day when he was reading the newspaper on his bed, he said to her, "Look, it says here, 'Chuck should marry Debe.' What do you think?"

They didn't tell anyone until one August day, I got a call from Dad saying, "Debe and I are in Las Vegas, and we just got married." I was stunned. What? You're kidding. Wait a minute. Not my dad. Dad continued his news with pride. "Yep, on a Harley, at a drive-up window, for thirty dollars." He was very proud of how cheap he was. He was not a big spender on such things.

A Brief Moment in Time

Dad decided to take Debe on a delayed honeymoon around the world in twenty-six days on a chartered *Concorde*, a British-French turbojet-powered, supersonic passenger jet airliner that flew at 1,354 miles per hour. This was the trip of a lifetime.

The creator of Aussie Shampoos was among the passengers on this voyage and asked Dad about his house and presumed second home. Dad laughed and joked that all he had was a small, crappy condo, thinking he was really something special. This did not impress the successful businessman, who said, "Don't you want a place all your kids and grandkids can get together? A place for the family to come and build memories?" A good question.

Dad hadn't thought of it that way before. When he came home from the world tour, he realized he'd just sold a rental building. This meant he could do a 1031 exchange and get another rental property. Where would it be? The choices were narrowed down to Hawaii or Colorado. He found the perfect place in Beaver Creek, Colorado, because he was told it was kid friendly and he was starting to have grandchildren!

He told everyone he'd bought a small condo, nothing big. When entering the lobby, you got on an elevator and the door opened straight into the condo entry and living room. A series of vast windows overlooked the entire side of the mountain, with white, picturesque ski slopes beyond. The view was breathtaking. Dad loved seeing the look on everyone's face as they stepped out of the elevator into the condo and their jaws dropped. Another favorite story of his.

He had bought it fully furnished because that was much easier than figuring out what to get. It was decorated in Ralph Lauren green, red, and plaids. The two bright green couches had the most uncomfortable and scratchy pillows on them. An original Native American painting that covered one entire wall gave all the grandchildren the creeps because of the way the man in the picture looked at you. Down the hall was the kids' bedroom that slept all eight of them in three bunkbeds and two pullout beds. This was perfect. All but the one bath for eight kids, but it didn't bother the parents. You didn't really want to enter the room because it was a disaster! It also had a huge dining table that could seat the entire family if we squished together.

The condo turned out to be a wonderful place for all of us to go, and over the years we spent lots of Christmas seasons there. The kids built forts, played Legos, games, and cards, and the girls made up dances to songs and performed them for all of us.

The skiing was the best! It was ski-in and ski-out, which made it super easy for all of us. We would come and go as needed. Often the guys left early to hit the black diamond runs, and the rest of us lagged behind not much before 11 a.m. The kids would switch from skiing to snowboarding, and we'd come in for lunch and try to go back out. Often, we couldn't get off the couch. We nicknamed the condo "the drug den" because as adults, you just wanted to relax, lie around, and do nothing.

Grandpa was proud of his grandchildren skiing, and they loved it when he opened his legs wide and they got to duck and ski between them.

When the kids were first learning to ski, we'd sit and look out our window and search for our child in ski school learning how to ski down the bunny slope. They'd come in a single file line, doing the snow plow or pizza, as we called it, with their skis. They'd be freezing from the cold and snow but having a wonderful time. We'd be sipping our coffee, in our cozy fuzzy socks. A nice break for the moms.

We'd walk or slip down the hill, depending on what shoes you wore, going to the square to shop or ice skate on the outdoor rink. This was where my daughter, Shannon, started her skating, at two and a half years old (real lessons started at four years old). Now she is an incredibly graceful national competitor and has all her triple jumps. She has skated in Beaver Creek's Thanksgiving and Christmas shows as one of the featured skaters, with thousands of spectators watching her perform.

Every year Beaver Creek has a World's Best Chocolate Chip Cookie Competition, and the winning cookie gets to be the official cookie of the mountain for the year. Everyone, especially Dad, loved the homemade chocolate chip cookies a chef, complete with his chef's hat, gave away each day at 3 p.m. at the bottom of Centennial chair lift.

The Aussie Shampoo creator was right. How special it was to have a place we could all get together and build wonderful family memories that we'll cherish forever.

Finally, a House for Debe

In 2007, Debe finally talked Dad into buying a wonderful house in Atherton, California. I think he bought it because he liked the fountain in the front yard. It offered great photo opportunities, with gorgeous trees and water cascading down several levels of rocks. It was surrounded by grass and held a reddish-purple maple tree. It was a beautiful single-story home with a guest house, pool, and a huge yard filled with flowers and tall trees. Everyone loved this secluded oasis.

(1995) Dad and Debe drive-up wedding chapel

(2005) Beaver Creek: Dad and Shannon

He Loved Us!

Knowledge is power.
Francis Bacon

Dad loved Debe, but he loved his kids too. His actions spoke loudly of his love for us. He built the King Empire so that we benefited. Over the years, he did so many things with us and for us. These stories are written here and into our hearts.

He proudly displayed drawings of each grandchild on his office wall. Dad especially got a kick out of his oldest grandchild Will's drawing. Dad went through a period when he got all new teeth. Will was pretty young and drew a family picture that included Grandpa with an arrow pointing to his big teeth. I think his favorite, even though he wouldn't pick favorites, was the picture of his Porsche 928 that Sam drew; Dad hung it in the family room.

Wherever you turned in Dad's house you ran into photos of the family; his refrigerator, tables, and walls were all filled with our stories.

I felt Dad's love when he flew my brothers and some of their kids on a chartered jet to watch me compete at my first USA Masters Track and Field Championship at the University of Oregon, my alma mater. It was awesome having my family there to cheer me on and support me. To encourage me to get over the high jump bar and break the world record for women forty to forty-four years old. What a treat.

Dad would always share his wisdom and knowledge whenever we asked. He'd help us if we had problems with a building issue, needed help selling a company, had a financial question . . . He had a wealth of knowledge that he was always willing to share with us.

He wanted all of us to grow up to be productive people who worked hard, were honest, had good character, and treated others with respect. He gave Connor and Shannon the DVD of the movie *The Ultimate Gift*, which says, "Life is how you live it . . . not how you spend it."

In his last year, he often told us how proud he was of us and how much he loved us.

Dad wasn't perfect, but he cared for all those around him. He wasn't always good at showing it. You had to look carefully. He was incredibly kind. He was a good man.

You now have a glimpse into the early years of the complex man we all loved dearly and who loved us dearly. Now we can move on to the rest of the story.

(2014) Will, the butler and Grandpa Charlie

(2005) Dad's seventieth birthday: The King family

The Impossible

When you have nothing to say, say nothing.
Charles Caleb Colton

The Camel Can't Fit

The definition of character: doing what is right when nobody is looking.
Chuckism

I first became a Christian before college and later read the Bible verse, *"It is easier for a camel to go through the eye of a needle than for a rich man to enter the Kingdom of God"* (Matt. 19:24). I was crushed because I immediately thought of my dad.

I know a camel can't fit through the eye of a needle. They are just too big! Okay, slightly! So why is entering the kingdom of God so difficult for a rich man?

Is it because they love money more than God? Maybe they have no need for God? Do they rely on themselves? Do they trust in their money? Is it pride? Is money what's most important to them, or making money? Is it greed? Is it a heart issue?

It could be one or a combination of those things. All I know is, as the saying goes, death and taxes are the only two certainties in life. So why put your trust in money? Its benefits are only for a short time. You can't take your things with you. You can't buy your way into heaven or by your good works get to heaven.

I know there are many rich men in the Bible that God blessed. So how does that happen, given the camel and needle thing?

I tried to talk to Dad. He humored me by listening politely from his "throne" as his enthusiastic daughter read the Four Spiritual Laws pamphlet to him. It talked about how Jesus is the bridge from sinful man to God in heaven. Afterwards, he didn't say much and went on his way as always. It left me thinking, *How will my dad ever enter the kingdom of God?*

I needed to pray. I spent thirty-five years praying for him. Also, my family, girlfriends, kids, and Bible study group have all prayed for him over the years. My girlfriend Diane wanted to send him a thank-you present after a girls trip we took skiing in Beaver Creek. I said, "He doesn't want anything. How about you send him a nice letter and pray for him? That's what he needs."

How could he enter the kingdom of God? I felt like he was too rich, too old and stuck in his ways to look toward Jesus. This seemed impossible.

Stripped Clean

When a foot compares itself to a yard,
it always comes up short.
English Proverb

The Almighty Dollar

For everyone to whom much is given,
from him much will be required.
(Luke 12:48, NKJV)

If you look in the dictionary for the word "risk-taker," you just might see a picture of my dad. He often walked a thin line in the business world. He was incredibly honest, squeaky clean, and did everything "by the book." However, where others might be more conservative, Dad was willing to go out on a limb and risk a lot. This was part of why he was so successful.

Dad often said, "One of the reasons I was so successful was because I surrounded myself with incredible people and partners." However, there came a time when he didn't listen to them. He felt he was unbeatable in the stock market and ignored everyone's advice, including attorneys, accountants, financial advisors, and even his own kids.

When I was growing up, he used to tell me, "Never invest in the stock market because it's too risky." Ironically, from around the age of seventy, all of his investments were in the stock market. Most people would have taken a portion of their money and invested conservatively. Not my dad; he was addicted to the deal. He loved the risk.

Prologis, a REIT (Real Estate Investment Trust Company), bought one of the companies Dad had sold. This purchase included a trade of several million shares of their stock, which became one of the top-growing stocks in 2006. It was valued at around seventy-six dollars a share.

In 2007-2008, with the local and national economy in a freefall, Dad began getting margin calls from UBS Bank. He had "leveraged" (similar to borrowing) money using the Prologis stock as collateral so he could invest the money elsewhere in the market. This wasn't a little bit of money. This was a significant amount of money—millions of dollars. Think of a number and keep going—that number isn't high enough.

It happened so fast that everyone close to him felt sick. Our heads were spinning as the stock spiraled down to $2.50 a share. Dad was forced to sell all his stock to pay UBS back. Everyone was stunned, especially my dad. He had lost approximately 97 percent of his wealth in a very short amount of time.

That'll change your life. But every almighty dollar he lost wasn't going to be as bad as what was coming next.

Vitality

Better life through chemistry.
Chuckism

*If you don't take care of your body,
where are you going to live?*
Chuckism

Dad was devastated. He'd lost most of his financial portfolio. Still, he had enough to live on comfortably. He no longer felt free to use chartered jets whenever or wherever he wanted. This had been his favorite splurge over the years. This financial loss, although on a grand scale, didn't need to affect his entire life. He was concerned for Debe's future if something were to happen to him. The reality was she would have been well provided for.

About this time, Dad's lower back began to hurt. He saw a few doctors and did a little bit of physical therapy but not consistently. I always asked him for the diagnosis but never heard what it was. He didn't seem to have answers.

I'm not sure which drug came first, but it opened a door in his life to the world of oxycodone/oxycontin (an opioid) and whatever drug cocktail he could talk doctors into giving him. He persuaded one doctor to exchange two-hundred-pill refill prescriptions for the use of his condo in Beaver Creek. Friendship at its finest.

In addition, there were sleeping pills, antidepressants, anti-anxiety medication, blood pressure medication, cholesterol medication, and other pharmaceuticals. He called his bowl of pills his "Garden Salad" because of all the colors.

In early 2008, I sat in on a round table meeting with my dad, Debe, brothers, accountants, and attorneys and expressed my concern that he was addicted to pain pills. No one wanted to believe that—not our Dad. Unfortunately, it didn't take long before Debe called me. She was worried he was going to overdose in the middle of the night. He was clearly addicted to the OxyContin pills.

Most of us have a picture in our minds of the stereotypical drug addict: someone who looks terrible and has bad teeth, shoots up heroine, steals money from family, and behaves badly. That wasn't Dad. He was a wise, silver-haired, seventy-three-year-old man who had experienced many amazing things in his life and imparted much to those around him. He was a father and grandfather to many. How could this happen?

I have since learned that this epidemic is now being called Opioid Use Disorder by *The Diagnostic and Statistical Manual of Mental Disorders*, Fifth Edition (DSM-5). This is a medical condition characterized by a problematic pattern of opioid use that causes clinically significant impairment or distress.

When I read the check sheet available in the manual about the disorder, it rang true of Dad. I think we on the outside looking in think, *Why can't he just stop? Why can't he choose something else?* He needed to make the decision to get help and stop; we couldn't make that decision for him. Struggling with this mental disorder, I don't think he could have done it alone. Unfortunately, Dad was not the only one with this problem.

Not long after Dad became addicted to oxycodone, Debe also became addicted to pain pills as a result of several botched oral surgeries. She lay in bed all day "napping," absent and unavailable to her daughter and granddaughters. She had waited her whole life to be a grandma. It used to be so important to her before opioid painkillers took everything she once valued. At one time she was taking eighteen different prescriptions. They changed her, sucked the life out of her. She had been an amazing painter. She painted stools for each grandchild, and she was incredibly crafty. Now that stopped too. To those of us who loved her, it made no sense at all. We could only shake our heads in bewilderment.

Dad and Debe slept their days, months, and years away. Often Dad wouldn't get out of bed until after two in the afternoon. He created what he called "The Bat Cave." It was a dark bedroom with blackout window shades, which he never opened, and he slept twenty-one or twenty-two hours a day. If he had opened those shades, he'd have found the most beautiful property surrounded by many rolling mounds of lush green grass and glorious rose bushes that were every color of the rainbow and smelled sweet and amazing. There were tall trees, a pool, and a large water fountain that filled the air with the sounds of a river in his back yard.

But sadly, Dad's drug-influenced decision was to live in darkness. When I entered the room, it felt like a dreary cave. Because he rarely got out of bed during the day, he broke down his expensive Tempur-Pedic mattress in less than a year and wore a huge chasm on his side of the bed, which didn't help his back problems. He was lost to us for years.

When we came to visit, we had to let him know we were coming over so he could make sure he was awake, and usually he wouldn't take a pain pill before we came. We'd sit on the couch and talk for an hour or so. Not much fun for the seven- and eleven-year-old grandchildren. Then he'd say, "I need to go to bed and take a pill." Sometimes I wouldn't even see him because he was still sleeping. I'd sit on the couch waiting and waiting. It broke our hearts to watch him care so little for life.

Sometimes my children, Connor and Shannon, convinced him to walk around his house or property, and yes, he always wore his slippers. Dad would ask them about life, and they'd talk to him about going into rehab at a place called Passages in Southern California. Dad always thought this was my idea, but it was theirs. They had seen it on television somehow. He would listen to the kids and say, "I'll think about it."

For several years he had worked with a personal trainer who came to his home with fitness equipment in her truck. That ended now too.

The drugs also aged them. Shannon thought Grandma Debe was eighty-five years old, but sadly she was only fifty-five.

There were countless calls to 911 from the house in Atherton, California—sometimes monthly. Atherton is home to some of the most expensive properties in the country because of the high-tech industry, including Google, Facebook, and Apple. The emergency teams were patient, but they often gave my brothers a look that communicated what we were all thinking: "What are these people doing? They live in this unbelievable home and could have anything they want. This is the life they are choosing? To not live at all?"

They spent days at a time in the hospital having tests and seeing doctors, but typically nothing more than dehydration was discovered wrong with them. Debe often had lung and breathing issues, and she was on oxygen for long periods at a time—even though opioids supposedly aggravated this problem. It was an endless cycle.

This was a sad existence for a man and a woman who used to live life and were once so happy together. Instead, they had chosen the prison of their bedrooms. Their world shrank, and now they avoided most social gatherings, often using the excuse that they weren't feeling well or were sick.

How much of this new conflict and Dad's actions were related to depression? He was very depressed and didn't know how to handle the emotions of his loss of money. He didn't really seek consistent help or treatment for his depression. Yes, he was on antidepressants, but he needed more help than pills could offer. I guess his answer, not a good one, was in the pain pills. Pain and depression, it all blended together.

On one occasion, the police found Dad around 2 a.m. in his Porsche 928 on the side of the freeway with four flat tires. He was clearly under the influence—loopy and slurring his words. He thought he was picking up Debe at the airport. Later, he didn't remember anything from that night.

But yes, that wise, silver-haired man, our dad, had forever changed. It was not how he raised us. I hadn't had many disagreements with my dad over the years, except in the early years over boyfriends. Okay, I'll admit it, he was right. I started having lots of stressful conversations mostly about money with him. He said things that were pretty harsh to my brothers and me. We have to remember it was always during the pill-induced state he was in.

There was a period where I didn't even want to talk to him on the phone because I was worried about what he was going to say to me or ask me. Once, when I was with him, I got so upset I went running out of his house in tears, unable to believe what he had asked of me. I collapsed sobbing in the arms of Charlie and Leslie.

My brothers met with Kristina Wandzilak (the addiction specialist from the television series *Addicted*). They discussed having an intervention but decided against it.

Thankfully, Debe decided on her own to go for treatment at the Betty Ford Center, an addiction treatment facility, in January of 2012. This made a big difference, and she began improving, yet she still had problems and wasn't completely healthy.

Ultimately, Dad was upfront about his situation. He was also very clear that he did not want to stop taking the pills. Dad's use of drugs resulted in a terrible loss of self and of what was truly important. The grandchildren had very little relationship with him since 2008. It was not a great way for them to remember their Grandpa Charlie. A tragic loss of vitality.

Shannon, Theo, Trish and Lola

(2015) Talking life with Shannon

(2010) Dad, Debe, and Porters'

My Guys

Loss is part of our journey.
Chuckism

Shannon and I were driving home to Albuquerque after skating in Colorado Springs because I had to do a television and radio interview. The Olympics were starting the next day, and we often did interviews since I was a member of the 1988 U.S. Olympic Team, and my husband, Pat Porter, was a two-time U.S. Olympian and eight-time consecutive U.S. National Cross Country Champion.

I saw on my phone that channel 13 was calling, so I answered it, figuring they too wanted to interview me. It was going to be a busy few days, I thought.

On the other end of the phone I heard a female voice say, "Can you please confirm your husband, Pat Porter's, plane went down in Arizona?"

At that moment, I couldn't breathe and started to panic. Tears were flowing, and I needed to think. *How can I think? What do I do?* I abruptly hung up the phone. My heart was broken. I pulled the car to the side of the road, got in the backseat with Shannon, and prayed. In an instant, my world was changed forever and would never be the same.

It was devastatingly true. On July 26, 2012, Pat, my husband of twenty years; Connor, my beautiful, funny, sweet fifteen-year-old son; and Connor's close friend Connor Mantsch passed away in a private plane crash. Pat was the pilot, and they had gone on a "boys' trip" to Sedona, Arizona—a trip from which they never came back. I had lost half my family, my guys.

Even though we lived in Albuquerque and Dad lived in California, he was very close to Connor. I was so thankful Dad got to see him two weeks before the accident. Over the years, Dad did several special things with Connor.

They stayed overnight at a llama farm, rode a tractor, and went to a kids' science discovery museum, the zoo, miniature golf, and Disneyland together. They had gone shooting and enjoyed talking guns and politics. Connor was super special. He won everyone's heart with his smile, sense of humor, affection, and love for the Lord. Especially Grandpa Charlie's.

Once, when they went skeet shooting in ninety-degree weather, Dad's Porsche heater got stuck on high. For the entire forty-five-minute drive there and back, they baked like burnt toast.

Dad challenged Connor with the M&M's compound interest project. Connor got twenty M&M's, and if he didn't eat them that day, Dad doubled the amount the next day. Connor ended with over three hundred M&M's. (I wish the bank gave that kind of interest on my money.) This also taught him about delayed gratification.

Pat had loved Dad like a father. They were very close and shared a passion for flying, guns, fast cars, and Harley-Davidson motorcycles. We built many memories traveling on our Harleys together throughout the United States and Canada. In the early years, Pat always enjoyed hanging out on Dad's bed, which is what you had to do if you wanted to talk to him. They talked hobbies, and before we were married, one day Dad mentioned to Pat, "I've always wanted a .357 Magnum Colt Python gun." Pat happened to have one, and the next time we saw Dad he gave it to him. Dad was like a kid and was thrilled. I think it was really bribery so Dad would like him and let Pat marry me. Which he did!

Dad once asked if Pat got into flying because of him, but he didn't. Pat had wanted to fly before I ever met him. He had tried to join the military to fly, but he was too old.

However, Dad's pain pill use left Pat incredibly frustrated and unable to handle Dad's change in behavior. Dad often wouldn't return Pat's calls. Once he even said, "What do I want to talk to him for?" This hurt Pat deeply and resulted in a broken relationship. Another tragedy of Dad's opioid use.

Dad didn't handle death well, so Pat's and Connor's death was exceptionally hard for him. He called me time and again, crying so hard I could barely understand him. This wasn't easy for me as I was just trying to survive myself. I needed the strength of my dad, but it wasn't there. It was lost in the bottle of pills.

My father was fifteen minutes late for their Celebration of Life service. I needed someone to prop me up, to be strong and help me get through one of the most difficult days of my life, but that wasn't him anymore. Dad's strength was lost.

(July 2012) The Porter Family

(2012) Last time with Connor

(2003) Connor and Dad shooting

(2001) M&M's compound interest: Connor

(2012) Celebration of Life: The Tucker family (Dad's sister)

The Love of Dad's Life

Time is like land. There is only so much of it.
Chuckism

Debe sounded like she had so many times before when she wheezed and struggled to catch her breath. With the roar of sirens and the glare of flashing red lights, the ambulance and police cars once again raced toward Atherton Avenue. They always arrived "just in time" to take Debe or Dad to the hospital. But this time there was no "just in the nick of time." There was no breath left. The EMTs couldn't give back her life.

On March 27, 2016, Dad's beloved wife of twenty years died suddenly in her room with Dad watching desperately from the bedroom door as they tried to revive her.

Debe was gone. Dad, Debe's daughter, grandchildren, and stepchildren would all miss her smile, her laughter, and her fun, playful, and creative spirit. We held her in our hearts as we held the photo albums she so lovingly made each of us. There would be no more.

This was NOT how life was supposed to be. This was NOT the plan. Debe was sixty, twenty years younger than Dad. She was supposed to take care of my dad and, in his words, "change his diaper when he was old." That was the deal. We all thought Debe would outlive him by many years.

I flew out to be with Dad the day after Debe died. I was all too familiar with this dark valley of grief and loss, and I understood Dad's pain.

When I went to check on him in bed, he asked me for some lemonade in his freezer cup (that's how he liked his juices). He said he didn't need a straw because he already had one that he had used before. When he went to put his straw in his juice I said, "Wait a minute." I noticed the straw was all black. Gross, it was filled with black mold. How long had he been reusing it? No wonder he had been sick and couldn't get better. His nightstand even had black mold on it from all the spills.

As I was cleaning up Debe's room, I found her Bible on her nightstand. My heart leapt when I opened it. It was filled with sticky notes, handwritten notes in the margins, quotes and lessons learned, underlined passages, and personal prayers. It was like the velveteen rabbit, tattered and worn but loved. It was real.

This was the Bible of someone who clearly loved the Lord although she never attended church. I knew then Debe had joined Pat and Connor, and one day I would see her again. Debe was in heaven.

(2008) Dad and Debe; © Jeanne L. dePolo

Purpose

Never give up! Never, never, never, never, never.
Chuckism

Dad didn't know what to do without Debe. He kept the 24" x 30" poster of her smiling face from the funeral on a bench next to his bed so that he could see her easily. It was heart wrenching. After some time, several of us tried to convince him to remove it. However, it was his favorite picture, and he wouldn't entertain that idea.

He decided it was easier to stay in bed in a drug-induced state than face reality. He had been in this place for so long. He felt guilty for her death and said he had no reason to live. Since he had lost his money and started using opioids, he had felt like this before. It wasn't new. But now we really didn't want to lose him after losing Debe. Everyone around him tried to convince him that life was worth living. He was loved and adored by his three grown children, ten grandchildren, step daughter, and all of their spouses.

Since Dad was a workaholic, it was tempting to think he should never have retired in the first place. Work was all he knew, and he had forgone all of his hobbies years earlier. Perhaps he just needed to replace one kind of work with another.

He felt he couldn't start a new business or a new relationship, claiming he was too old and didn't have the energy. He had no hobbies, so what was he to do? He felt he had no value. He talked about this often. It seemed he was stuck.

Of course, none of this was true. It was all a lie he believed and nurtured. This was not the father who told me all those inspirational sayings such as, *"We move in the direction of our uppermost thoughts."*

He could have fed into his grandchildren's lives more. He could have been a mentor to young business-minded kids or volunteered—the list was endless. He was a man who'd achieved so much, yet now he felt he had no purpose. He had no hope.

People in God's Plan

Friendship is the only choice in life that is ours.
Tequila Sunrise (1988)

A Godsend

It's always easier to ask for forgiveness
than to ask for permission.
Rear Admiral Grace Murray Hopper

Charlie, Leslie, Mike, and Annalisa had helped take care of Dad and Debe for years, bringing them whatever was needed, limiting their access to pills, having them over for dinner, taking them to doctors, going to their house when the police called, and so much more.

Sometime after Debe's death, Charlie and Mike recognized they needed part-time help. Charlie hired Beth Ann, his wife's good friend, to help with Dad and give him his medications. Charlie told her, "Now you'll probably always see him in his underwear and no teeth." Because that's how he'd been living. Surprisingly, that almost never happened. Dad's assistant, Erin, said, "He'll do anything for a pretty girl." Even get dressed! We were all relieved. Especially Beth Ann!

She came several days a week for a few hours a day. She took copious notes on the amount of medicine he took, the food he ate, what time he woke up, and how much exercise he got. Given that Dad's idea of exercise was walking from his bedroom into the kitchen and then back to bed, his level of activity was totally pathetic.

Beth Ann did an amazing job. Over time, she decreased his pill intake, especially the opioids, and got him eating real food (as opposed to ice cream and Ensure). He called her "The Nazi," but eventually he thought she was okay. She had him on a new pre-sleep routine, which included relaxation techniques and drinking tea before bed. He was sleeping better. This meant he stopped taking additional sleeping pills when he woke at 6 a.m. in order to sleep all morning. He got up at a reasonable time each day for the first time in nine years.

Beth Ann gave him things to look forward to. She had him going to the grandchildren's events: Evan's football and Grace's volleyball games. He even watched my daughter, Shannon, practice her ice skating. When we came to visit, he'd take us to lunch (we drove) at the Dutch Goose for his favorite bacon cheeseburger and deviled eggs. It was nice to get him out of the house.

When taken on regularly scheduled outings to Charlie's or Mike's house for dinner, Dad wasn't in a hurry to leave like before. He was more engaged and involved than he'd been in years.

With all this new activity, Dad occasionally forgot his teeth! Like a good son, Charlie would race back to Dad's house to get them in order to spare him the humiliation of looking like a homeless person. I'm not sure Dad really cared, but Charlie did.

Beth Ann would come over and make Dad dinner because she wanted him to eat and didn't want him to be alone. She even convinced him to help her in the kitchen. He said he hadn't eaten so well in thirty years, not since my mom cooked for him. Once he told her, "Don't tell Charlie; he says, 'I've never seen Dad eat a green vegetable.'" She got him to eat berries for breakfast every day. Fruit . . . I'm sure his body went into shock. Quickly she added, "Now, they did have the biggest pile of whipped cream on them. Much more cream than berries." He used so much whipped cream she bought it in bulk.

Beth Ann saw that he got dressed up for Mike's fiftieth birthday party. He looked so handsome in a blue suit coat with a handkerchief in his pocket. We will disregard that he still wore his slippers.

Dad was diagnosed with breast cancer and started going through all the tests and doctors' appointments associated with cancer. His mother and grandmother had both died from breast cancer. Dad did not want to get treatment for his cancer.

Beth Ann was truly a godsend and a tremendous blessing who encouraged him each day as she too had successfully walked this journey. Plus, she talked about spiritual things with him. She was part of God's plan, and we are forever grateful to her.

We know that because of Beth Ann, Dad lived a better life for over a year. We could enjoy him far more than we had in a long, long time. This meant time for making new memories with all the grandchildren and time to ultimately see God's plan play out fully. A new, more hopeful part of the puzzle of Dad's life was now being placed together. Thank God for Beth Ann.

Beth Ann, "The Nazi," a godsend

(2016) Evan's football game: Grace, Charlie, and Leslie

(2016) Shannon's skating practice: Mom and Dad

(2017) Dad ready for Mike's fiftieth birthday

A Gift from God

When God closes a door, He opens a window.
Oscar Hammerstein

One of my favorite pieces of the puzzle is shaped like a heart. I hadn't dated in almost three years. I wanted a man who loved the Lord and was athletic, kind, and funny. (Of course, there was more to my list, but I was trying to leave it in God's hands.) A hard combination to find, and I think many people thought it was impossible. I was waiting on God. A first for me!

Now, I left it in God's hands, but I was proactive in some ways too. I thought if anyone could introduce me to someone, it had to be my friend Dale because he knew everyone in town. I told Dale, "I give you an 'F' for not introducing me to someone." Dale is the husband of one of my best friends and a partner with the largest architectural firm in New Mexico. He was slightly surprised and taken aback, but he kept it in the back of his mind.

Finally, he had someone for me to meet—James. They had known each other for about thirty years through business, and Dale felt we might be a good match.

As I walked up to the restaurant with butterflies in my stomach, a beautiful double rainbow was visible over the restaurant. I believed the double rainbow was for me, and our first date was off to a great start!

James had lost his wife of thirty-three years the year before we met. He too was familiar with loss and grief. Dad often told people how much he missed Debe, and then he'd say, "You don't understand." He couldn't say that to me. To me he'd say, "I know you understand." He also couldn't say it to James—the only man in his life who deeply understood his pain and the guilt that comes from losing someone prematurely and feeling you should have done more.

Dad really liked and respected James. Before recently retiring from corporate management, James enjoyed a successful career as a partner and senior vice president of community development and planning for one of the top engineering firms in New Mexico.

When we talked on the phone, Dad always said, "Say hi to James for me." I took this as a good thing. Unfortunately, Dad often found it hard to remember some family members' names.

Four months later, to my excitement and joy, I became Mrs. James Topmiller. I also gained his two incredible adult children, a daughter-in-law, and now an adorable baby granddaughter.

Wow! This is only a small piece of the puzzle of our love story. It was an amazing example of how God works things together for good. I'd love to share all the details, but that is for another time. I never could have imagined how God would use this new puzzle piece.

I am so thankful I waited for the right man, who loves the Lord. God did exceedingly and abundantly beyond all that I thought possible through James. What a gift!

(2016) James and Trish Topmiller

Persistence Pays Off

The mind is like a parachute.
It doesn't work until it's open.
Frank Zappa

For years when I visited Dad in California, I'd ask him to go to church. For many years, he wasn't getting up until one or two in the afternoon, so going to church with him wasn't going to happen. But I'd often invite him. I'd talk to Leslie and my brothers and encourage them to keep inviting him as well. They'd say, "We do, but he never wants to go." I thought he'd never go. He always had an excuse.

He didn't grow up in the church or want to talk about God. He had no interest in spiritual matters, which is how he'd been his whole life.

Who wants to keep asking someone when they always say no? After Debe died, Leslie and Charlie started regularly asking him to go to church. To our astonishment, one day he actually said yes and started going to church with them weekly. They didn't give up. Thank God!

The "Angel"

People are too busy looking at themselves
to look at you.
George Navone

At times, it's hard to believe how God works—and often in ways I never thought possible. I've seen this several times throughout my life, but I believe this time was a miracle.

God sent an angel to the church Dad was attending. Seated in the second row of what used to be a subdued and conservative congregation was Michael, a lovely spirit-filled man who entered into worship with his whole being. Often lifting his hands in praise, he swayed to the music and sang with his whole heart.

Dad was inexplicably drawn to Michael, often calling Charlie midweek to ask if they were planning to go to church on Sunday. Imagine my dad, who lived on "King Standard Time," telling my brother that he wanted to get to church early because he wanted to "sit behind the black man, my friend." My father, the man who NEVER wanted to go to church, was suddenly going out of his way to go to church and be near his friend Michael—a man I believe to have been an angel sent by God. God uses the unexpected!

I'm reminded of the verse: *"Do not neglect to show hospitality to strangers, for by this some have entertained angels without knowing it"* (Heb. 13:2).

A wildly unexpected piece of the puzzle had just been placed. A man was set into Dad's life who showed him what it looked like to worship God with his whole mind, heart, and spirit. How exciting!

Boldness

There are some things that people are going to have problems with, no matter what you do.
Chuckism

Way to Go, Charlie

If we don't try, we won't succeed.
Chuckism

Over the years, Charlie and Leslie were examples of the love of Christ, and they witnessed to Dad through their lives. They had many conversations with him about their faith as well.

Soon, Charlie felt it was time to talk to Dad about Jesus. This took courage, strength, and deep love. I know this because over the years my attempts to talk to Dad about Jesus fell on deaf ears. He felt no need. He thought he was a "good person." He'd donate money to reputable causes, and he thought that was all he needed to do. He thought it was enough.

Charlie asked, "Dad, do you want to pray to receive Jesus?" Dad replied, "No." So much for Charlie's boldness. Dad wasn't ready yet, but Charlie had planted a very important seed, which gave God the chance to water and make it grow.

Little did Charlie and Leslie know that God was using their faithfulness and love to prepare Dad's heart for the visit still to come.

Charlie loved Dad. Way to go, Charlie.

Charlie's Angel

Faith is evidence you can't see.
Chuckism

The next Sunday at church, after Charlie talked with Dad about having a relationship with Jesus, he talked to Michael the angel. Charlie said, "My dad really likes you. He wants to go to church early every week now because he wants to sit behind you. Would you mind talking to him about Jesus? I tried, but he said no." Michael's simple but totally unexpected response was, "God's got your dad in His hands!"

Okay, really? What person who loves Jesus doesn't say, "Absolutely. I would love to talk to him for you"? Charlie left, shaking his head and not really understanding. But Michael already knew that God had Dad in His hands. We didn't know what to believe or think.

My Plan

If you want to make God laugh, tell him what you're doing tomorrow.
Chuckism

A few days later, while we were in Albuquerque, I said to James, "You need to talk to Dad when we go visit him next week. You need to tell him about Jesus. It needs to be you. You are the best person to do this." I was very matter-of-fact but insistent (or stubborn, as my dad would say).

James, not convinced, responded, "I'm not even sure I'll have a chance to be alone with him." I emphatically replied, "No, no, you are the one. You need to do this. Please. I'm sure of it. Okay, we will pray and get others to pray."

James was at a business meeting when I told our couples Bible study group about my plan. They agreed to join me in prayer. When James came in later, the other men patted him on the shoulder and said, "It's your job to share with Trish's dad. We will be praying."

James, thinking that Dad was a bit intimidating, thought for a while and then shook his head with a smile. "God has to go before me to prepare his heart. If God wants this to happen, then God will open the door for me. My prayer is that when it's opened for me, I'll be faithful to enter it."

Later, James told me that he wasn't fearful about the task put to him but was internally acknowledging the enormity of the situation.

We began praying for James's time alone with Dad. That's the power of prayer and faith—faith that we have a big God!

"Minor" Details (Not!)

Life is about making smart choices, not fast choices and not easy choices.

Chuckism

To Stay or Not to Stay?

It's easier to stay out of trouble than
to get out of trouble.
Warren Buffett

I hadn't stayed overnight at my dad's house in years. Sometimes being there meant trouble. It was very hard for me to be around him when he slept all day. We'd had several confrontations that left me feeling upset, sick, and frustrated. He acted the total opposite of how he'd raised me and how he used to be. Looking back, I'm sure he didn't remember any of the confrontations because of all the drugs.

We were going to see Dad for his eighty-second birthday. James thought we should stay with him to be close, so I mentioned to Beth Ann that we were coming. But being in the main house with Dad was not typical. I used to stay in the guesthouse if I spent the night. However, Debe's daughter and son-in-law had divorced a few years before, and the son-in-law was living in the guesthouse. Dad enjoyed the occasional company and yummy meals he cooked.

Beth Ann decided to set up a guest room in the workout room of the house. She did a lovely job making the space ready by placing gorgeous, fragrant roses from his garden by the bed and in the bathroom. The treadmill was where we put our luggage. We knew we needed to stay at Dad's house. God was taking care of the seemingly "minor" details.

Later Is Better!

Excellence is not a singular event, but what you continuously do as a habit.
Shaquille O'Neal

When we visit my family in California, Shannon usually skates early in the morning in San Jose at the Sharks' workout rinks. This trip was one of the only times she ever skated later in the morning because that's when the choreographer could work with her. I'm all in for later, not early. We got to sleep in, much better than a 5 a.m. wake-up.

With Shannon and me gone for several hours that morning, James had the time alone with Dad that we had prayed for back in Albuquerque. This was a unique opportunity that had never happened before. Puzzle pieces continued to "fall" into place. A God thing, for sure.

The Way

If you don't run the race,
you have no chance of winning.
Chuckism

God Leads the Way

*You can catch more flies with honey
than with vinegar.*
English Proverb

James was intentional but knew God needed to lead the way. As he thought about this, he decided to do his morning Bible study on Dad's kitchen table at nine o'clock, just in case Dad came out. Remember, there was a time when Dad didn't come out until one or two in the afternoon.

James set out some food that Beth Ann had prepared. Beth Ann had also prayed, knowing James was hoping to talk to Dad. When Dad came into the kitchen, James asked him to join him for some breakfast. Dad usually stood at the counter to eat, but today he sat down while they talked for a bit. "I hear you're going to church," James said. Dad replied yes. Then he told James about the black man, his friend.

James told Dad he was studying the Bible that morning and asked if Dad ever spent time there. Dad said no. James then shared what he was studying about and the impact of the Bible in his own life.

He said he had a question for Dad and asked, "If you were to die today and you were at heaven's pearly gate and were asked, 'Why should I let you into heaven?,' what would you say?"

Dad responded the way James thought he would: "I've been a good person."

"By whose standard are you good?" Sometimes, a short, direct question said in the right tone of voice will be taken well. James continued. "That's the problem. In heaven, with God, the standard is perfection, and we aren't perfect. No matter what we do, we all fall short, miss the mark, sin. Our sin separates us from God." James then asked Dad, "Have you ever told a lie?" When Dad said yes, James explained, "That's just one example of the sin that separates us from God."

"For all have sinned and fall short of the glory of God"
(Rom. 3:23).

"For the wages of sin is death"
(Rom. 6:23).

"We (mankind) started off in a perfect relationship with God. We lost that relationship, because of sin. Our once-perfect relationship with God was now broken."

James noticed that Dad kept moving closer and closer to him as they talked. Finally, Dad said, "Hang on. I need to get my hearing aid." James wasn't sure what to think and wondered how much Dad had really heard. However, he felt that Chuck had been responding well up to that point. Moments later, Dad came back to talk and hear more.

James is an extremely good listener and asked Dad about Debe. Dad really opened up, sharing his pain, how much he missed Debe, and what a good wife she'd been. He spoke about how much he'd loved her and how much she'd loved him. He also talked about the guilt he felt. James understood Dad's loss.

He shared about the loss of his wife Linda, what life was like after her death, and how Linda was truly in a better place.

James asked if Dad knew where Debe was today, in heaven or not? Dad said he was sure she was in heaven. James then asked him if he wanted to see her again someday. He wanted to see her.

They talked about the Bible, God, Jesus, purpose, and their lives. James told Dad about the time recently that he and his own dad talked about purpose in the later years of one's life.

Dad didn't typically talk very long with people, especially about personal things. He'd say, "Okay, I'm done now. I have nothing more to say." I often heard these words from him after just a few minutes of conversation. But James and Dad talked for a couple of hours. That was a miracle!

Finally, he asked Dad, "Would you like to meet Jesus and restore your relationship with God?" Dad hesitated. James, not wanting Dad to close the door prematurely, continued talking and listening. God had been waiting for my dad. James could wait too.

Trish Goes the Wrong Way

If you want to get a job done, look for the busiest person you can find.
Chuckism

James and Dad needed more time, so God got me out of the way. That was clearly needed.

Shannon and I were on our way home from skating when James called. I had him wait a second because I was getting onto the freeway, and I wanted to concentrate. James asked me if I knew where we could get Dad a Bible. I was excited! We spoke for a second, and then James continued his visit with Dad.

I've driven Interstate 280 my whole life. But it was April, and I was driving along the freeway thinking, "Wow, it's really green on these hills. I don't remember it being so green when I drove this road yesterday. Hmm, I don't recognize these exits. That's weird. I must not be paying much attention usually on this drive. Hmm."

I knew this route and should have been off the freeway in seventeen minutes. However, thirty minutes later, I realized I was going the wrong direction on a totally different freeway, I-680 across the Bay! Now I had to take Dumbarton Bridge to get home.

Really? Had I really driven thirty minutes in the wrong direction? Who did that? None of it made any sense except that

God turned wrong things into good things for His purpose. It meant James had well over two hours (an extra hour) to be with Dad. Clearly, I hadn't needed to be there, and James had needed to be alone with Dad. God was in control.

Dad Finds the Way

If you don't like the answer, ask a different question.
Chuckism

James continued talking with Dad and explained, "The good news is that even though we aren't perfect, God has provided a way for us to be in heaven with Him someday. It's not based on how good we are. He sent His Son Jesus Christ to die on the cross for us and for our sin to restore our relationship with God. Anyone who believes in Jesus will be saved."

James again asked Dad if he'd like to pray together and sincerely place his trust in Jesus. This time the response was different. Dad said yes!

Together James and Dad prayed, asking God to forgive him of his sins, professing that he believed in Jesus Christ, and putting his trust in Him.

After they prayed, James gave Dad a piece of paper with the prayer. He explained what this new, restored relationship with God would mean for his life—a new life in Christ. Everlasting life!

How exciting for those who loved him. James knew I would be thrilled. This was all God! This was a piece of the puzzle that I never thought I'd see. That I thought was impossible. Thank You, Lord!

It's True. It's Real.

What we do for ourselves dies with us.
What we do for others remains forever.
Chuckism

Chuck's Bible

Tell the truth and you won't
have to remember your lies.
Chuckism

We wanted to give Dad a Bible right away, but we couldn't find a store nearby. We called our close friend Angela in Albuquerque because we knew she could help. We asked her if she would choose a Bible for us, have Dad's name engraved on the cover, and then overnight it to us so we could give it to him before we left the following day. Engraving usually took a week, but an exception was made for Angela. She was able to ship it later that day.

The Bible arrived the next morning. It was beautifully bound in the softest black leather. It had the words of Christ in red and study notes to help make the Bible more understandable. As requested, "Chuck King" was engraved in silver on the cover.

When I saw the Bible, disappointment flooded me as I realized I should've had Dad's full name engraved on it— Charles W. King, Jr. I thought I'd blown it and was frustrated with myself, but I'd forgotten that God was in control. God had a plan.

James, Shannon, and I presented it to Dad the next morning. He was happy to get it and immediately started looking through it. Where should he start? We told him the book of John was the best place for a new Christian to start reading the Bible because it tells the story of Jesus. James flipped to the book of John, in the New Testament, and put a sticky note on it that read, "Start here!"

Then he suggested Dad put his slip of paper with the prayer he prayed in his new Bible.

I told Dad one of Connor's and my favorite verses was John 3:16: *"For God so loved the world that He gave His one and only begotten son, that whoever believes in Him shall not perish but have everlasting life."* James said it was also his favorite verse. So he put a sticky note by the verse and wrote, "Trish, Connor, and James's favorite verse."

Shannon said, "My favorite verse is, Jeremiah 29:11: *'For I know the plans I have for you, declares the LORD, plans to prosper you and not to harm you, plans to give you hope and a future.'"* So we put a sticky note there saying, "Shannon's favorite verse."

I said, "Oh, my other favorite verse is Romans 8:28: *'And we know that in all things God works for the good of those who love Him, who have been called according to His purpose.'"*

James put his arm around my dad and said, "You see, Chuck, if I hadn't gone through that really tough time in losing my wife, I never would have met your wonderful daughter or her wonderful dad." Just as all the angels in heaven were rejoicing, I too was over the moon with excitement. I knew many others would be joyful when they heard this great news. My heart was so full.

Church Alone

People don't change as they grow older; they only
become more like themselves.
Chuckism

Beth Ann told me Dad was really into going to church now and even went alone twice, without her or my brothers. This was a little scary as I wasn't sure he should have been driving. We noticed his car had new dents and scratches all along the side of it. Oh my, but he wanted to go to church!

This meant he had to wake up early, get out of bed, get dressed, drive to church, park, walk inside alone, find a place to sit . . . Beth Ann felt that Dad was seeking and listening to God's words, and he was making that happen ON HIS OWN, without anyone. It made her heart happy to know he was welcoming God.

All of this took determination and effort from a man who had never gone to church during his life. It also required a new heart. That blew me away.

Hands Raised

Never be afraid to try something new.
Remember: Amateurs built the Ark.
Professionals built the Titanic.
Dave Barry

Leslie told me about one of Dad's last times at church. It's how she wants to remember him.

As usual, Dad requested that they sit behind his friend Michael. As the worship band played, Dad stood. Michael often circled his arms and, at the end of the song, circled just one hand while slowly and audibly saying, "Thank you, Jesus!" Leslie was stunned when Dad raised his hands like Michael with a huge smile on his face. Dad looked over at Leslie with a look of joy and surprise, almost as if he couldn't believe what he was doing.

I would've given anything to have seen my eight-two-year-old dad waving his hands in church. I would never have thought that possible. *Oh, you of little faith!*

I remember how hard it was for me the first time I raised my hands in church. I felt awkward and incredibly self-conscious. Dad was neither. He was freely present in the moment. Was he glimpsing something we couldn't see? Was he given a glimpse of heaven? Was he given grace to see those who had gone before him? I wonder. The only thing I know is that my dad, Charles

W. King, Jr., praised the Lord freely and unashamedly, just like Michael the angel. This was confirmation. He loved Jesus! Jesus was real to him.

Final Things

Happiness isn't about the things you have,
but rather the ability to enjoy what you have.
Chuckism

Take Control

Don't worry about the things you can't change.
Dr. Larry Deitz,
from the book It's Not What I Know . . .
It's How I Learned It by Richard B. Liposky

On Wednesday, August 2, 2017, Beth Ann texted me that she had just refilled Dad's Oxycontin prescription, and Dad was asking to have control of the pills. Over the past year, she'd been distributing them to him as needed. Beth Ann was concerned, but not as concerned as other times because he was doing so much better.

He was awake more and started using a Fit Bit (exercise step tracker). When he started exercising, he was walking 750 steps a day and had increased to 2,500 a day in less than three weeks. (On a side note, medical professionals recommend doing 10,000 steps a day for a healthy life. Dad wasn't even close to that number). Dad was very numbers driven and goal oriented, so this was motivating for him.

I called Dad right away. We usually didn't talk for more than a few minutes, and I didn't have anything exciting to tell him. In the end, I said, "I love you," and he said, "I love you more." What sweet words. Plus, he told me, "You know how important you three kids are to me. You are my whole world." As he talked, I wrote down the words. "I love you more."

He sounded good . . . maybe too good. I texted my brothers, "I just spoke to Dad, and he sounded really chipper."

Chipper was not a word we'd usually use to describe my dad. I meant he was "too chipper," but I didn't say that. Charlie and Mike didn't feel an urgent need to call him right away. They lived near him and saw him regularly, so they probably figured they'd see him soon enough. Understandably, in hindsight, I felt bad that I wasn't clearer.

The Choice

*We move in the direction of the
uppermost thoughts in our mind.*
Chuckism

Thursday morning, August 3, 2017, I got the heartbreaking call from Leslie that Dad had passed away. He had taken his life the night before by ingesting almost the whole bottle of Oxycontin pills. Tragically, he became an opioid overdose statistic.

What had controlled so much of his life now killed him. His need for risk-taking and the adrenalin rush that came with the high of the deal. He couldn't figure out how to live life without it. He felt he had no purpose.

We all knew he was depressed. Dad was seeing a psychologist, and the week before he had changed Dad's medication. Was this a factor in his choice? We don't know. I do know one of the side effects of antidepressants can be suicide.

Depression and opioid use disorder are both mental disorders. We can judge someone and say, "Why don't you just quit? Why can't you get better?" But we haven't walked in their shoes. Sometimes it takes the family being proactive and getting help for their loved ones. Sometimes it doesn't work out how we thought it should. I wish we could have done more. I wish he had gone into rehab. He was doing so much better, we thought.

When someone dies by their own choice, it usually leaves those left behind with all sorts of questions and unresolved feelings. What more could we have done? How did we fail? Those are all natural feelings.

Dad inadvertently sent the message that we weren't worth living for. That the Jesus he trusted in and the God he had begun to worship were not enough to justify life. He was too caught up in this life, and his pain, to open his eyes and see the number of people he would dramatically impact and negatively affect by his choice. But we also need to remember how unwell he had been and the tragedies he had endured. We need to view him this way. He did love us. He wanted the best for us.

There was so much more he could have done, so much more life to live and people to impact. He could have been an example of growing old gracefully. He could have shown all of us what it looked like to follow God in our old age with new purpose. There were so many of us that still needed him. This ending wasn't God's best. The sad part is that all the people who loved him are left hurting and missing him. The good news is that he is no longer lonely, hopeless, or in pain.

As I look back on how goal oriented Dad was, I wonder if his new goal had been heaven—to be reunited with those he loved. Now he is walking on streets of gold, seeing the face of Jesus, and singing songs of worship. He is catching up with Debe, Connor, and Pat. He is with God!

Charles W. King, Jr.

April 18, 1935-August 3, 2017 - Eighty-two years old

(2005) Dad, Mad Hatter hat

(1993) Dad on his Harley

God Keeps Working

If you don't look, you won't see.
Chuckism

Something Unexpected

Give a man a fish, and you will feed him for a day.
Teach a man how to fish,
and you will feed him for a lifetime.
Chinese Proverb

In the middle of the next night, I was startled awake and wondered what would happen to Dad's Bible. Then a peace came over me. "Charlie gets it. It has his name on it."

When I woke up in the morning, out of the blue, James asked, "Who gets your dad's Bible?" I told him, "Charlie. It has his name on it." A smile crossed my face as I remembered how bad I'd felt when I realized I didn't put Dad's full name on the cover. That oversight was unexpected but worked out for the best.

I spoke to Leslie that morning, and she told me Charlie had gone into Dad's room looking for a note but didn't find one. Instead, he found Dad's leather Bible with "Chuck King" on the cover. My brother had been called "Chuck" most of his life. However, a few years before, he'd begun using "Charlie" at work so people wouldn't confuse him with Dad. Charlie opened the Bible and thought, *This is a really nice Bible. I've never had a Bible like this.* He took it home. I'm sure Charlie looks at that Bible today as a memento of Dad and how he came to meet Jesus.

Thanks, Dad, for giving Charlie a new Bible to cherish.

I am in awe of how God cares for every detail—even the name on Dad's Bible. Every piece of the puzzle was important.

What's Really True?

What's the difference between
"the wise man" and "the clever man"?
The clever man gets out of situations
that the wise man never gets into.
Jewish Proverb

Purpose in Life

A believer's value and purpose never end. There was so much more in life Dad could have done.

He didn't know what was going to happen the next day. He might have felt differently or had a new goal. Dad deprived himself of the opportunity to find out what a new day might bring. The Bible says joy comes in the morning.

Michael Wasn't Really an Angel?

Some have questioned the story of Michael the angel, thinking he was not an angel. Maybe. It's certainly possible, even probable perhaps, he wasn't an angel. Michael may have only been a human being like the rest of us. An imperfect man, one who doesn't "have it all together," who doesn't have a full knowledge of God's ways and may not understand everything in the Bible correctly. Funny, it kind of sounds like most of us.

However, for a short period of time, it is abundantly clear that Michael was God's messenger to my dad. The Bible tells us over and over again about deeply flawed (but God-loving) men being used by God (Samson, Paul, David, Solomon . . .).

Michael, whomever he is, was used by God for the benefit of my dad. To me he was definitely an angel.

Taking One's Life

There are those who believe that because Dad ended his own life, he is not in heaven. I, along with many other Christians, don't believe this is true for one moment.

According to God's Word, suicide is not what determines one's entry into heaven. John 3:16 says belief in Jesus is the only way: *"For God so loved the world that He gave His one and only begotten son, that whoever believes in Him shall not perish but have everlasting life."*

Another Bible verse says, *"For all have sinned and fall short of the glory of God"* (Rom. 3:23). We don't measure up to God's standard. No one does. Taking your own life, though serious (and a form of murder), is just one type of sin. You and I have our own areas of sin. Thank God that, in spite of our sins, He can still save us believers through Jesus. Our sins are washed away, forever forgiven and forgotten.

Romans 8:38-39 reads, *"For I am convinced neither death nor life, neither angels nor demons, neither the present nor the future, nor any powers, neither height nor depth, nor anything else in all creation, will be able to separate us from the love of God that is in Jesus Christ our Lord."*

Therefore, because of Jesus Christ's death and resurrection, nothing can separate believers from the love of God! Jesus died for all of our sins. In a time of spiritual attack and weakness, if a true Christian commits suicide, his sin is still covered by the blood of Jesus.

Was He Really Saved? Was He Sincere?

There are those who question whether Dad was really saved, especially since he killed himself. I'll respond by saying, who are we to judge whether someone who has professed Christ is saved or not? Only God knows!

Yes, we all wanted him to say, "I want to live now. I want to go out and have a productive end of my life for Christ." Maybe we just wanted him to leave church each week saying how powerful the message was and how it affected his life.

What do we expect from an eighty-two-year-old man who seldom, if ever, shared deep feelings and really was handicapped when it came to interpersonal relationships and communicating? God looks at the heart, not at the outside things.

But We Didn't See a Total Transformation

Who of us has "total transformation" just after meeting Jesus? Yes, a few might, but we all still must fight against fleshly sinful desires. But let's look closely at Dad.

His Bible was on his bed off and on, which suggested there were times he was reading it. God sent an angel with the message, "God's got your dad in His hands." He was eager to go to church each week and wanted to be on time. Frankly, that's a miracle in my book. He verbally confessed his belief in Jesus. He went to church on several Sundays, and two times in a short period of time he went by himself. As I said earlier, this meant he got up early, got dressed, drove to church . . . Finally, he raised his hands and worshipped the Lord with his whole body moving to the music.

Each event standing alone is perhaps inconsequential, insignificant. But taken together, in contrast to his life prior to meeting Jesus, the message is loud.

I'm reminded of the story from the cross. Two criminals hung on a cross on either side of Jesus. One recognized Jesus was being punished unjustly and said, "Lord, remember me when You come into Your kingdom." *"Jesus answered him,* 'Truly I tell you, *today you will be with me in paradise'"* (Luke 23:42-43). This criminal had little time to show his change to others, but he showed it to Jesus as they hung together on their crosses. His life was over, yet he went to heaven because a few minutes before he died, he believed in Jesus.

I am going to choose to believe the Bible: "If you declare with your mouth, 'Jesus is Lord,' and believe in your heart that God raised Him from the dead, you will be saved" (Rom. 10:9).

Yes, Dad is in heaven today because we have a just and merciful God who loves us.

"I write these things to you who believe in the name
of the Son of God so that you may know
that you have eternal life."
(1 Jn. 5:13, NIV)

The Puzzle Box Top

As I look back at Dad's last years, I realize his life was like a complicated jigsaw puzzle. There were so many individual pieces that didn't necessarily make sense or seem to fit at the time. However, now I see each piece fit perfectly in its own place.

I didn't know what the final picture looked like because I couldn't see the top of the puzzle box. The top that showed the whole picture at one time. Only God could see it. What we viewed as tragic events and heartaches, or insignificant occurrences, God was able to ultimately use for good. This was Dad's life puzzle, now fully complete.

In a sense, Dad set the example for us. He showed us and others that meeting Jesus is important, even in our old age, to the shock or disbelief of others.

There is a puzzle related to each of our lives in the Lord. After the loss of Pat and Connor, I stood on, "I trust you, Lord!" That was how I got through each day. Four years later I still couldn't say, "God is good!" On my first date with James, I asked him how he was doing after the death of his wife. He said, "I'm fine. God is good!" Wow. The one phrase I couldn't say was what James stood on. He filled in the gap where I was unable to. God was working in my life.

I was also unable to say that God could use the loss of Connor for good. My fun-loving, incredibly special, happy boy. It couldn't be possible. But because of Connor's and Pat's death, I've had opportunities to share my story with many people. Maybe it inspired them or brought them hope. I was planting seeds, little bits about Jesus over the years. No big harvest or anything too exciting . . . except to God.

If I hadn't lost Pat and Connor, I would never have met James. Maybe Dad would never have come to know Jesus as his Savior. Thankfully, I know that Pat and Connor were already saved. Connor especially, with his heart for others, would have freely given his life for his friends, family, and his grandpa. Maybe in some sense, Connor did indeed give his life for his family. We still marvel at Shannon's letter she wrote in the program for the ice skating tribute to Connor, soon after he died. She promised Connor that she would stay true to God in remembrance of him.

All these pieces of the puzzle are hard to wrap my brain around, but I am grateful how they came together. The pieces fit!

It's Possible

With man this is impossible, but with God all things are possible.
(Matt. 19:26)

Being truly rich has precious little to do with dollars and cents.
Chuckism

Earlier I mentioned the Bible verse, *"For it's easier for a camel to go through the eye of a needle than for a rich man to enter the Kingdom of Heaven"* (Matt. 19:24).

Well, interestingly enough, in the very next verse, the disciples asked, *"'Who then can be saved?' Jesus looked at them and said, 'With man this is impossible, but with God all things are possible'"* (Matt. 19:25-26).

God saved my father. A rich man on earth, now an even richer man in heaven (true riches). Rich on earth means material wealth, but we can't take things to heaven with us. True riches are our relationship with Jesus Christ and eternity in heaven. People and our relationships are also what's valuable. Whatever we possess in this life, whether on earth or in heaven, is all a gift from God.

We can't save ourselves. We're not good enough, rich enough, or smart enough. It is impossible for us, but not for God. God answered our years of prayer. God did what I thought could never happen. God looked beyond Dad's wealth, and tough exterior, into his heart. There He saw Jesus. Dad no longer worshipped the money he'd been given on this earth, but he now worshipped God, the source of true riches.

What about being too old or too late to meet Jesus? These terms mean nothing to God. If you don't believe in Jesus, it's generally true that the older one is, the greater the callousness and hardening of the heart toward God's calling. However, unless your conscience is totally seared, God never stops calling you, seeking you, drawing you toward Him. The Bible says, *"He has put eternity in their hearts"* (Eccl. 3:11, NKJV).

Dad felt that calling and responded to it in a saving way. He didn't reject it. God saved him because he believed that God could save, even him. Never too old. Never too late.

Does any of this suggest that we should live in a worldly, ungodly manner and then turn to Christ in the last days of our life? No! First, do you know when you are going to die? Connor died unexpectedly and at a young age. Remember, God laughs when we tell Him what we are doing tomorrow. Second, do you really want to delay the joy and purpose found by knowing and serving God today? Do you really want to reject the only true God of this universe, your Creator? Do you really want to risk missing a glorious eternity in heaven?

Let's say I'm wrong. If so, nothing significant is lost. But if I'm right, then you have a lot to lose. Eternity with God.

It's beautiful and amazing the way God used so many circumstances and people to bring this one rich, self-centered man into His Kingdom—a seemingly impossible task, a needle's eye too small, a puzzle too difficult. But God loved my dad enough to send His Son Jesus to die for him. God loved him enough to pursue him to his last days.

He loves you too! His love and grace might be the one thing you need. My prayer is that God will continue to use the story of my dad and that Dad's story will speak to your heart and help you to realize you need Jesus too. He is waiting for you to come to Him. Never too late, never too old, never too rich, never too . . . anything!

"He (God) gives us more grace" (Jas. 4:6). To some, meeting Jesus might seem farfetched, ridiculous, and impossible. But we know that it's not. We know that when we need it most, God gives us more of what we need. You can know this too because you now know the story of my dad meeting Jesus. Dad listened to God. He took the step of faith in Jesus Christ. How about you?

What Else Would You Expect?

You never get a second chance
to make a first impression.
Will Rogers

At Dad's burial, James and I were early—only because of James. I still run on "King Standard Time" (although not two hours late, just late).

While we were waiting for everyone to arrive, I got a text from Debe's daughter, saying, "I'm caught in traffic and am late." I replied, "No problem." Then I got a text from Mike's wife, Annalisa, saying, "We will be late. Lauren [their daughter] got her car locked in the parking lot at school because she was leaving early for the service." I responded, "No problem." Then Leslie called me and said, "Charlie is late because of traffic and something with the motorcycles."

I smiled and thought, *It figures. Why would we start on time for Dad's burial? That's so Dad!*

One More Thing

Financial success can add pleasure to things and objects but can't nourish the soul.
Chuckism

The last time Leslie went to church with Dad, they had to go to their satellite church, The Café. Tatiana, the singer at The Café, had a beautiful voice. The week after Dad passed away, Tatiana was leading worship in the main sanctuary for the first time. Before she sang, she talked about laying down and letting go of whatever we may value more than Jesus.

Then she sang the worship song "Crowns" by Hillsong Worship, which talks about your wealth being found in the cross. That your greatest crown doesn't have value anymore. Not wanting anything more than Christ and the cross.

In his final months, Dad felt he had nothing left to offer. He often recited the same mantra, beginning with, "There's nothing left for me to do. I started three companies, I . . ."

As Tatiana began singing the song that day, Leslie felt a powerful presence reassuring her that the words in the song's chorus echoed how Dad now clearly sees that all of his accomplishments were never what Jesus sought. Jesus just wanted Dad's heart. Now Dad understands.

Always Be Prepared

It never hurts to ask.
Chuckism

It's important to understand about sharing Jesus with your friends, family, and those God brings across your path. Here are seven steps that will help you be intentional and prepared for sharing Jesus and His love with others: **pray, be prepared, be watchful, walk through, be loving, be bold,** and **ask.**

Pray

Pray that God will prepare your heart and the person you want to share Christ with. God hears our prayers: *"This is the confidence we have in approaching God: that if we ask anything according to his will, he hears us"* (1 Jn. 5:14).

Pray that God will go before you, prepare the way, and prepare their heart. That He will open their eyes to see Him. That you will be bold to walk through the open door if He gives it to you. Get others to pray too. There is power in praying together.

Be Prepared

Have a plan. Think ahead. Know the "Roman Road":

- *"For all have sinned and fall short of the glory of God"* (Rom. 3:23).
- *"For the wages of sin is death"* (Rom. 6:23).
- *"God demonstrates His own love toward us, in that while we were yet sinners, Christ died for us"* (Rom. 5:8).
- *"For everyone who calls on the name of the Lord will be saved"* (Rom. 10:13).
- "If you declare with your mouth, 'Jesus is Lord,' and believe in your heart that God raised Him from the dead, you will be saved" (Rom. 10:9).

It's okay if you don't know each verse perfectly by heart. I've been amazed how I can botch things, but God still works in the person I am talking with.

Be prepared to share your own life, testimony, and how God has worked in your life. Do you clearly know your testimony, and have you practiced it? *"Always be prepared to give an answer to everyone who asks you to give the reason for the hope that you have"* (1 Pet. 3:15).

Be Watchful

If you have prayed and prepared, then wait and be open to God working. Watch to see if God opens a door. The Lord gave instructions to Habakkuk to *"Look at the nations and watch— and be utterly amazed. For I am going to do something in your days that you would not believe"* (Hab. 1:5). Look and you'll be surprised at the doors He will open for you.

Walk Through

If God opens the door, you need to walk through it. Make the most of the opportunity He has given you. How will you know the door is open? As you've asked questions and are listening to how they respond, watch for any spark in the person's reply or a comment in a spiritual direction. If there is, then you can move forward. Ask more questions. Ask about their objections to faith. Ask if you can try to answer any questions they may have. You just need to be faithful and continue. *"When you are brought before synagogues, rulers and authorities, do not worry about how you will defend yourselves or what you will say, for the Holy Spirit will teach you at that time what you should say"* (Luke 12:11-12).

Be Loving

Have an attitude of love. The rest of 1 Peter 3:15 is, *"But do this with gentleness and respect."* Really listen to them. Ask questions kindly. Be prepared to stop sharing Jesus verbally if they aren't ready and get offended or get aggressive. Have a heart of love.

Be Bold

Don't be shy. Don't be apologetic. Be confident and excited about this "Good News." Be bold with what Christ has done in your life and who He is. Share your testimony. *"He proclaimed the kingdom of God and taught about the Lord Jesus Christ—with all boldness and without hindrance"* (Acts 28:31).

Ask

Remember to ask if they would like to pray to receive Jesus' salvation and forgiveness. In sales they call it "asking for the close." You'd be surprised at how many gospel-sharing people don't ask this simple question.

Why don't we ask if they'd like to believe in Jesus as their Lord and Savior? Maybe it's because we worry about what the person will think; we don't want to offend them; we don't want to be pushy, and/or we are scared to ask. *"If you remain in me and my words remain in you, ask whatever you wish, and it will be done for you"* (Jn. 15:7).

Have you practiced the words of the prayer that God wants to hear?

Remember, *"He has also set eternity in their heart"* (Eccl. 3:11, NASB). I love this because even as we are worried about sharing Jesus with them, God has already prepared them for Him and for our conversation.

Ultimately, it's God's timing. We are planting seeds, and God waters the seeds. It is not our job or responsibility to force or coerce someone's personal commitment to Jesus Christ. That choice is up to them. Know that God is already at work in their lives. We don't know where the person we are sharing with is in his/her journey. Only God knows. Don't be discouraged. Keep praying for them. Keep being an example, light in the darkness, city on a hill, and more. Keep loving.

Now that you are ready to share Jesus with someone, let's see in more detail how to help someone meet Jesus.

How Do You Meet Jesus?

*We should live our lives with the understanding that
we are going to die.*
Chuckism

Let's imagine you died today and arrived at heaven's pearly gate. If you were asked, "Why should I let you into heaven?," what would you say? If your answer is, "I am a good person," that won't work. You can never be good enough. If your answer is, "I've done terrible things, and God would never let me in," that's not true either. You may have done some bad things, but that's not what finally matters. "I go to church. I'm a member of this religious group or denomination." Religion won't save you. Neither will going to church every week or donating money to charity.

Let's consider what the Bible says about the pearly gate question.

Truth: God Loves You

God made you with a void in your heart only He can fill. He is pursuing you and wants you to be in heaven with Him forever. *"For God so loved the world that He gave His only begotten Son, that whoever believes in Him should not perish but have everlasting life"* (Jn. 3:16).

Problem: Everyone Sins against God

God's standard is perfection because He is perfect. We aren't perfect. We all fall short and miss the mark. We all sin. Mankind started off with a perfect relationship with God, but they lost that relationship because of sin. Have you ever told a lie? Have you ever been unkind? Greedy? Hateful? These are just some examples of the sin that separates us from a perfect God. *"For all have sinned and fall short of the glory of God"* (Rom.3:23).

Consequence: Our Sin Separates Us from God

Man's once-perfect relationship with God is now broken. Separation from God (spiritual and physical death) is the penalty of our sin. *"For the wages of sin is death"* (Rom. 6:23).

Solution: God Gave Us Jesus Christ

God sent His Son Jesus to die on the cross for our sins. His death paid the penalty for our sins so that we could have a new relationship with God and be with Him forever. *"God demonstrates His own love toward us, in that while we were yet sinners, Christ died for us"* (Rom. 5:8).

Our Responsibility: Believe in Jesus

If we sincerely believe in Jesus Christ, our relationship with God can be restored, and we can be saved from eternal separation from God. Believing in Jesus Christ is to trust him as your Savior. Believe who the Bible says He is, that He is God and He alone can save you. He paid the penalty for your sins, and you are forgiven. *"For everyone who calls on the name of the Lord will be saved"* (Rom. 10:13).

"If you declare with your mouth, 'Jesus is Lord,' and believe in your heart that God raised Him from the dead, you will be saved" (Rom. 10:9).

To Do: Pray

What can we do that allows God to restore our broken relationship with Him? Pray! Sincerely. Simply. How?

- Admit you sin against God.
- Ask God to forgive you of your sins.
- Believe in Jesus completely, especially His ability to save you.
- Be willing to turn away from sin in your life.

You could pray a simple prayer like this:

> *Dear God,*
> *I know that I have sinned against You. Please forgive me. I believe Jesus is Your Son, who died for my sins and rose again. Please come into my heart and life forever. Help me to live a life that pleases You. In Jesus' name.*
> *Amen.*

Let's go back to our original question. What is the answer to that pearly gate question, "Why should I let you into heaven?" You now know the correct answer: "Because I believe in Jesus Christ and He has saved me." If this is your answer, then you can boldly say you are a new child of God, your sins are forgiven, and you have received eternal life. Welcome to God's family!

You are part of God's family, so now what? It's important that you grow and continue to learn about Jesus. To get started, I suggest you go to a Bible-teaching church, read the Bible, pray regularly, join a Bible study, and spend time with other Christians. Wow, that sounds like a lot, but if you can connect with someone at the church, they should be able to guide you. Get to know God; get to know Jesus.

Hold on tight; the ride is only beginning! Woo-hoo!

Remember, when we believe in His son, God accepts us at all stages of life:

- Never too old
- Never too young
- Never too rich
- Never too addicted
- Never too poor
- Never too unlovely
- Never too bad
- Never too criminal
- Never too late
- Never too . . . anything

Almost There

Success is just a number of daily small victories.
Chuckism

More Information

Garbage In. Garbage Out.
George Fuechsel

Be Proactive for Your Health

I am a big believer in being proactive for your health or a family member's health. Not every doctor has all the answers, and sometimes it takes going to multiple doctors and different kinds of health practitioners: medical doctors, therapists, psychologists, nutritionists, or exploring the alternative medicine route. The point is to seek second opinions and fight for your health. You are worth it!

Opioid Use Disorder Checklist

Go to my website www.TrishPorterTopmiller.com for an Opioid Use Disorder checklist.

Review

Please review the book on Amazon.com if you liked it. I really appreciate it. Thank you.

Let Me Know

A truly wise man always has
more questions than answers.
Chuckism

James and I are always available to talk with you about Dad's story or how you too can have a relationship with Jesus Christ. Go to my website www.TrishPorterTopmiller.com to email me. We'd love to hear your comments, how this story impacted you, or if you too have recently met Jesus.

Blessings, Trish

About the Author

Best way to succeed—do what you're good at and find experts in other areas.

Chuckism

Trish Porter Topmiller is a 1988 U.S. Olympian in the high jump, former world record holder for women ages forty to forty-four in the high jump, and multiple times U.S. National and World Masters Champion. She is the author of the book *Rekindle Your Dreams*, in which she shares her insights into the practical steps for making dreams happen.

© Serge Timacheff

Trish has a bachelor's degree in business marketing from the University of Oregon. She is a frequent speaker and guest on radio and television programs and has been the subject of interviews in the *Wall Street Journal*, *USA Today*, *Today's Christian Woman*, and others. She has worked with the media promoting various sports events for over thirteen years and is involved in the Fellowship of Christian Athletes. She attends Woodmen Valley Church in Colorado Springs, Colorado, and Sagebrush Church in Albuquerque, New Mexico.

Trish lost her husband of twenty years (Pat Porter, two-time U.S. Olympic team member) and son Connor (fifteen years old, U.S. National Fencing medalist) in a plane accident in 2012 and recently also lost her father. She married James Topmiller in 2016 and has a wonderful daughter, Shannon, who is a nationally competitive figure skater.

For more information, go to: www.TrishPorterTopmiller.com

"King Not Here"

*Jesus answered him, 'Truly I tell you, today you will
be with me in paradise.'*
(Luke 23:42-43)

Today, if Dad's phone somehow rang again, I imagine it would go like this:

- The phone rings and rings.
- No one answers.
- The voice mail comes on with a new greeting.
- It says, ***"King Not Here. I'm in heaven with the King of Kings."***
- Click.

One day I'll join Dad again, sharing stories and experiencing the **Greatest Adventure of All**—eternity—with our heavenly Father and His Son Jesus.